Praise for Bret Lott (from reviews of *Jewel*)

letters & life

on being a writer,

on being a Christian

BRET LOTT

∷ CROSSWAY

WHEATON, ILLINOIS

"Why Have We Given Up the Ghost?" originally published in *Image: A Journal of the Arts and Religion* 43 (Fall 2004): 79–91.

"Writing with So Great a Cloud of Witnesses" originally published in *Image: A Journal of the Arts and Religion* 69 (Spring 2011): 75–85.

"Humble Flannery" originally published in *The Writer's Chronicle: The Journal of the Associated Writing Programs* 34.1 (October/November 2010): 18–23.

Cover design: Studio Gearbox

First printing 2013

Printed in the United States of America

Hardcover ISBN: 978-1-4335-3783-7
PDF ISBN: 978-1-4335-3784-4
Mobipocket ISBN: 978-1-4335-3785-1
ePub ISBN: 978-1-4335-3786-8

Library of Congress Cataloging-in-Publication Data

Lott, Bret.
    Letters and life : on being a writer, on being a Christian /
Bret Lott.
       p.   cm.
    Includes bibliographical references and index.
    ISBN 978-1-4335-3783-7 (hc)
    1. Authorship—Religious aspects—Christianity.
2. Fiction—Religious aspects—Christianity. I. Title.
PN171.R45L68   2013
814'.54—dc23   2012036922

Crossway is a publishing ministry of Good News Publishers.

TS		23	22	21	20	19	18	17	16	15	14	13
15	14	13	12	11	10	9	8	7	6	5	4	3	2

With thanks.

CONTENTS

The author would like to thank the editors of the
magazines in which these essays originally appeared:
"Why Have We Given Up the Ghost?"
and
"Writing with So Great a Cloud of Witnesses"
in *Image: A Journal of the Arts and Religion*

"Humble Flannery"
in *The Writer's Chronicle*

Now there are also many other things that Jesus did.
Were every one of them to be written,
I suppose that the world itself could not contain
the books that would be written.
John 21:25

Part 1

LETTERS

Why Have We Given Up the Ghost?

Notes on Reclaiming Literary Fiction

My name is Bret Lott, and I believe in God the Father Almighty, Maker of heaven and earth. And in Jesus Christ his only Son our Lord; who was conceived by the Holy Ghost, born of the Virgin Mary, suffered under Pontius Pilate, was crucified, dead, and buried; he descended into hell; the third day he rose again from the dead; he ascended into heaven, and sitteth on the right hand of God the Father Almighty; from thence he shall come to judge the quick and the dead. I believe in the Holy Ghost; the holy catholic church; the communion of saints; the forgiveness of sins; the resurrection of the body; and the life everlasting. AMEN.

So that's where I'll start this book.

I'd also like to start by saying that neither the title of this particular essay nor the book itself will be a sermon. Rather, it will be, as far as I can tell at this beginning of actually writing down what I think I want to say, an examination of my own story as a writer, and why this is a question that haunts me, no matter how many books I have written.

And what really is "literary fiction"? What I've always known it to be is fiction that doesn't sell very well. But when my students ask me point blank what the difference between popular and literary fiction is—and they ask this question a lot—I tell them that literary fiction is fiction that examines the character of the people involved in the story, and that popular fiction is driven by plot. Whereas popular fiction, I tell them, is meant primarily as a means of escape, one way or another, from this present life, a kind of book equivalent of comfort food, literary fiction confronts us with who we are and makes us look deeply at the human condition. Henry James said that it wasn't "the rare accident"—the plot—that made a story worth our attention but the "human attestation" to that plot: how people deal with their histories rather than those histories in and of themselves.

At least I *think* that's what is meant by literary fiction, and what I'll take it to mean here today.

All of which is to say, I'm still trying to figure this topic out, after all these years as a writer. How, I want to know, is it so very difficult to give God, in my work as a writer of literary fiction, his due?

I started this with the Apostles' Creed because I do believe in Christ's divinity, in his resurrection, in his being precisely who he claimed to be. That is, I believe in a supernatural God, one who loves us and who cares intimately and deeply for us, so deeply that he gave his only begotten son to die for us. And I believe in a supernatural God whose wrath, as my life's reference book—the Bible— tells me, will be inflicted upon this world so fully that John saw in his revelation "the kings of the earth and the great ones and the generals and the rich and the powerful, and everyone, slave and free, [hide] themselves in the caves and among the rocks of the mountains, calling to the mountains and to rocks, 'Fall on us and hide us from the face of him who is seated on the throne, and from the wrath of the Lamb, for the great day of their wrath has come, and who can stand?'" (Rev. 6:15–17).

That, folks, is the God I believe in. The loving God who loves us on his terms, and his only.

And now begins the rub of this all: despite the fact I get the feeling I may very well be preaching to the literary choir if you have begun reading this book, I feel pretty certain some of you out there must be asking yourselves right now, Does he really believe in the supernatural? Does he really believe that God asserts himself outside of our hands, outside of our control, outside of our concepts of time and space, to actually show himself to us?

Yes. I believe in a God who works outside of us all.

Let me tell a story now. Or two. Maybe three.

A few years ago I worked my way through the book *Experiencing God* by Blackaby and King[1]—and already I can bet I have fallen in the eyes of many out there: he did *that* book, the one everybody and his brother was carrying around back then? Next thing you know, he'll tell us he's read *The Purpose Driven Life*.[2] But I'm afraid it's even worse than that: I am an adult Sunday school teacher at East Cooper Baptist Church, a Southern Baptist church in Mount Pleasant, South Carolina, and I *taught* our class *The Purpose Driven Life*.

The fact is, I am about the squarest person you will meet. I was a cubmaster for seven years, assistant scoutmaster for three; I was an assistant soccer coach for eight years too. I play baritone sax in my church orchestra—not in the hip and cool praise band but in the orchestra. For several years my wife, Melanie, and I ran our church's Wednesday night supper. To reach even further back, and to see perhaps how *really* mundane my faith story might appear, I was born again after a Josh McDowell rally when I was eighteen years old and a freshman at Northern Arizona University, and I met Melanie—we've been married for over thirty years now—in the college and career Sunday school class at First Baptist Church of Huntington Beach/Fountain Valley in Orange County, California.

We are talking square here.

But to *Experiencing God*—one day the book instructed me to pray for an opportunity to share Christ in some way. I was told to pray specifically for an opportunity, and then instructed as well to keep my eyes and ears open, to look for that opportunity, rather than simply to pray it and forget it.

Later that day I was in my office at the college where I teach, and I received a phone call. It was from one of my students, a genuine slacker who hadn't shown up for class that day, a kid I had written off weeks ago. And of course you know already how this story will end.

But I want to underscore what a slacker this kid was and the attitude I had toward him. I don't dislike any of my students—I love them. Really. But there are certain kids who show up in your classes and you know by their actions how much they want to be in the class, and so you begin to adjust your own views of them to reflect theirs of you. That is, this wasn't a kid with whom I would have gone out of my way to build a relationship. He was simply marking time in my class, and so I was simply marking time with this phone call.

He was calling to say he was sorry for missing class and had some lame excuse for not having been there. I remember leaning back in my chair and putting my feet up on my desk, listening to the story and, the phone to my ear, rolling my eyes. I really remember rolling my eyes at this kid.

And then he said it: "Mr. Lott," he said, "if I were to read a book from the Bible, which one would it be?"

Just like that. Out of the bluest blue you can imagine, me already shining this kid on, rolling my eyes, marking time with him.

And I sat up, then stood at my desk, me hit square over the head with the two-by-four of God's answer to my prayer that morning: to receive an opportunity and to watch for it. Sadly, I had just about dozed off at the wheel but was blessed enough to have been awakened in time to recover myself and begin to talk about the Gospel of John but also about the book of Acts, my favorite. Oh, and James, too. But John. The Gospel of John.

And I saw, because I had been caught unawares, that this prayer wasn't about my giving the message of grace to someone I had signed off, but about my having signed him off: it is the *being ready* that mattered, I saw. The message of salvation saves in and of itself; opportunities abound every minute we are awake to share.

But it is being ready to do so that matters.

Of course, the enlightened among us will chalk up the outcome of that story to chance, to coincidence. Maybe even to a conniving kid who, knowing as most every kid on my campus does that I am a Christian, thinks he has found a way to appeal to my forgiving side if he intones inquiry into the Bible while asking to be excused from a class he has missed. Don't think this all hasn't occurred to me.

But I see, finally, that none of that matters. What matters is that that morning I prayed for something—an opportunity, and an awareness—and was provided with both when I was least expecting it. That kid had no idea, I saw, that I was praying for this, and though I have to this day no idea if he really read John or not, he was given by a willing messenger—me—an opportunity.

That is all God asks, I saw. That willingness from us.

And this opportunity given was a supernatural act, God's answer to prayer.

But here are the other two stories. A little more dramatic, I think, than the possibility of coincidence.

I have been on church missions trips to the Eastern European country of Moldova twice now, the first trip with my older son, Zeb, to help build an orphanage for kids in the town of Telenesti, the second time to help run a Bible camp for kids in the same town. Moldova is the poorest country in Europe—the average income there is $30 a month, this in what had been an industrialized Soviet bloc country.

My job this last visit—Melanie and both our boys came this time—was to be the activities director for the Bible camp. Here was my Cub Scout expertise, come back to haunt me: my job, given me by acclamation, was to herd 140 children ranging in age from four to eighteen into four groups and then to entertain them for four one-and-a-half-hour blocks each day for a week—all in translation, either to Romanian or Russian, depending on the age of the kids. I and my team organized games and sports for them all. The last day we did wacky relays—silly games such as standing directly over an empty soup can on the ground and dropping a clothespin into the can from your forehead, or skipping rope ten times, or kicking your unlaced shoe off your foot to see who could launch it the farthest. We'd brought our own supplies—those clothespins, empty cans, all sorts of arts and crafts supplies—everything from Polaroid film for pictures of the kids to T-shirts (140 of them) for the children to tie-dye one afternoon. The mission group—there were sixteen of us, all from East Cooper Baptist—spent an entire afternoon a week before we left parceling out all these supplies evenly so that no one was overburdened. There were even entire sets of Old and New Testament flannelgraphs, too, for the nationals to use once we got to the camp in Moldova, all parceled out.

One of the relay games was a goofy thing in which a kid runs to a paper bag, next to which are two garden gloves. The kid has to put on the garden gloves, then reach into the bag and pull out the pack of chewing gum inside it, and then extricate a stick of gum from the pack with these garden gloves on, put the stick in his mouth, take off the gloves and run back to tag the next person on his team, until everyone is done.

The problem we were facing all week, though, was the kind of problem we all wish for: there were simply more kids than we had been told would be allowed to participate. Simply too many kids. The first day we opened up, in a ruined school that in America would have been featured on national news for the scandalous fact that its broken and filthy shell still housed kids for classes, we had 170 kids show up.

And I'd packed only enough gum for 160 kids, thinking that twenty extra pieces—we were told there would only be 140, remember—was in fact planning ahead. So on that last day, going into the relays, I knew we didn't have enough gum. I knew it. But there had been no place to buy more, and so we simply went ahead with the game.

Zeb and Jake, my younger son, served as monitors, helpers of a sort for the smaller kids once they were down at the bags and trying to put on those gloves. And late in the day, once we were working through the last batch of kids, Zeb hollered out to me, "Dad, we're going to run out of gum!"

I hollered back to him the only thing I knew to do: "Pray!" I said, and prayed myself, that somehow there might be more gum, that this would work out.

Zeb prayed, too. As did Jacob, and Skip McQuillan, the other dad along, and his two sons, Sam and Mac. We all prayed there, on the spot, that somehow there would be more gum, enough for all of them.

And there was enough gum. To the person: precisely enough pieces of gum, at the end of a frantic day of wacky relays, just a crazy day spent doing crazy games as a means to entertain kids who were being brought the gospel message elsewhere in the school by the nationals for whom we were helping with this camp.

It is with a kind of wonder and joy that I tell this story, no matter the cynic in me—Satan, actually—who rationalizes that perhaps not every kid participated that last day, and maybe not every kid did the relay. But there were more kids that day than any other, and they all did the relay.

And if there had been some single kid who had come up to the bag and found there was no gum for him, where would God have been, finally?

I believe in a supernatural God.

One last story, this from that same trip. There's a little fact I left out of all this: two of our team lost their luggage altogether, traveling from Charleston, South Carolina, where we all live, to the capital city of Moldova, Kishnau. So that though we had spent all that time parceling out all our various supplies, it didn't really matter: we didn't have enough of what we needed.

Sure, Debi McQuillan, Skip's wife, had brought some extra Polaroid film, more than she'd passed out to us all, and there were, finally, plenty of ice cream sticks for the frames they would make for those photos. There was enough glue and glitter, enough of that Dayglo plastic string to make lanyards for them all. We made do with a couple of softballs and a baseball bat less than we had planned to have ready.

But the big craft event the last day was the tie-dyeing of T-shirts. And we'd packed 140 T-shirts. Enough for the number of kids we'd been told would be there. There wouldn't have been enough, not by a long shot, even for the number of kids we'd planned for. That is, there weren't even 140 T-shirts. Plain and simple.

And here's what we did: we prayed over the T-shirts. We knew we didn't have enough, and we prayed over them, and then stepped boldly into that last day's craft activities, faithful that somehow we would have enough T-shirts, though we knew we had less than we needed.

And at the end of that long day of messy crafts—imagine, to begin with, trying to guide that many kids at dyeing T-shirts twisted and rubber-banded into knots, and then not being certain who would get one and who wouldn't—at the end of that long day of stepping out in faith, *there were precisely enough T-shirts for every kid who was there—over 170 children.*

In the book of Joshua, God instructs Joshua to choose twelve men from the tribes and to have each one carry a stone from where they crossed the Jordan and place it where they were camped on the other side. "Pass on before the ark of the LORD your God into the midst of the Jordan, and take up each of you a stone upon his shoulder, according to the number of the tribes of the people of Israel," Joshua instructs them, "that this may be a sign among you. When your children ask in time to come, 'What do those stones mean to you?' then you shall tell them that the waters of the Jordan was cut off before the ark of the covenant of the LORD. When it passed over the Jordan, the waters of the Jordan were cut off. . . . So these stones shall be to the people of Israel a memorial forever" (Josh. 4:5–7).

These stories I have just given you are only a few of my own standing stones. They are reminders to me and to those who come after me—you reading this—of the supernatural power of God.

Because I cannot explain how we got the right amount of gum, or why a kid called me to ask what book of the Bible he should read on a day when I'd written that kid off, or how we got enough T-shirts to make each kid at that camp feel a part of that camp at the end of a week in which they were presented the gospel message. In the town of Telenesti, in the country of Moldova, there is no running water, there are no flush toilets. Needless to say, there is no Wal-Mart to which we could repair and purchase bundles of T-shirts to save the day. But in Telenesti, there were orphans, kids whose parents had left them outright simply to go somewhere else and try to live. And there were also kids who lived with their parents and who showed up to that Bible camp unannounced and unplanned for.

And not one of them went wanting. No one was missed.

I can only tell you that these standing stones point to a supernatural God, one I can't explain by logic or rationalization. I can only bear witness to him.

And now, finally, we come to the thin ice of my own believability as a human being, and at the same time the concrete foundation of what it means to have faith. Do I really believe that God reached out his hand to us and, as those five thousand people who'd gathered at Bethsaida on the shore of the Sea of Galilee were given food from five loaves and two fish, gave us some extra gum and a big wad of T-shirts?

Yes I do. Count on it.

For if I, as a believer in Christ as God on earth, can find a way to explain away a phone call or a pack of gum or those T-shirts, then what is the point in my believing in the resurrection of a dead man? Plain and simple.

But I do believe it. Plain and simple. Our God is a supernatural God.

I have a friend who is a surgeon. He too is a believer, and he told me one time that he has to be careful of talking about God and God's role in his life when he is around other surgeons. It's because no matter your skills as a surgeon, he told me, no matter what schools you went to, where you did your residence, *no matter how long you've been saving lives*, once your colleagues smell on you a belief in something outside of yourself, you will be thought of as a loose cannon. A nut. A surgeon's hands are his to maneuver, a doctor is taught, and to believe that there is any sort of supernatural element involved in your being a successful surgeon is to admit into the OR an unaccounted-for entity, and hence the possibility for error. It is to admit a vulnerability.

I believe the same thing happens in the world of literary art. We have become so primed to believe in the self that there is no room for anything else, that it seems preposterous to have characters whose lives are altered by a supernatural God. James Joyce took that word *epiphany*—the "shining forth" or revelation of God to man in the person of Jesus Christ—straight out of the church to slug in for his notion of the moment in a story when man's humanity, as it were, shines forth on himself, or on the reader. Ever since, when it comes to stories, that term *epiphany* has meant a kind of psychological reckoning of characters to themselves and their world.

Regrettably, we have no choice but to admit that literary fiction as we know it today is undeniably a product of the Enlightenment. In September of 1784, Kant wrote in his landmark essay, "An Answer to the Question: 'What is Enlightenment?'":

Enlightenment is man's emergence from his self-incurred immaturity. Immaturity is the inability to use one's own under-

standing without the guidance of another. This immaturity
is self-incurred if its cause is not lack of understanding, but
lack of resolution and courage to use it without the guidance
of another. The motto of enlightenment is therefore: *Sapere
aude!* Have courage to use your own understanding![3]

This definition sounds downright inspiring, employing as its assumptions—its beginning points—language that ties inextricably
a dependence upon the guidance of another with immaturity, with
cowardice and irresolution. Who wants to be immature, a coward,
indecisive? Who among us wants to be thought of as anything but a
thinking, courageous, *understanding* person?

But of course the Enlightenment led from one thing to another—
and I am fully aware of the historical leapfrogging I am doing here—
with each succeeding movement a movement, in the world's eyes,
forward, until we have arrived here, today, at a moment when ex-
istentialism—whether optimistic or pessimistic or simply refusing
to choose sides—has yielded an age in literature in which God isn't
just dead, but nonexistent. According to *The Oxford Dictionary of
the Christian Church*:

> The [Enlightenment] combine[d] opposition to all supernatu-
> ral religion and belief in the all-sufficiency of human reason
> with an ardent desire to promote the happiness of men in this
> life. . . . Most of its representatives . . . rejected the Chris-
> tian dogma and were hostile to Catholicism as well as Prot-
> estant orthodoxy, which they regarded as powers of spiritual
> darkness depriving humanity of the use of its rational facul-
> ties. . . . Their fundamental belief in the goodness of human
> nature, which blinded them to the fact of sin, produced an
> easy optimism and absolute faith of human society once the
> principles of enlightened reason had been recognized. The
> spirit of the [Enlightenment] penetrated deeply into German
> Protestantism, where it disintegrated faith in the authority
> of the Bible and encouraged Biblical criticism on the one hand
> and an emotional "Pietism" on the other.[4]

It is this notion of reason-centered pietism, as it were, that I believe rules the day in the world of literary fiction. Pietism that is reliant solely on the manifestation of what we have come to know as *compassion*, a word sorely misused for years as a kind of secular stand-in for the notion of grace in the God sense.

Flannery O'Connor writes in her essay "Some Aspects of the Grotesque in Southern Fiction":

> It's considered an absolute necessity these days for writers to have compassion. Compassion is a word that sounds good in anybody's mouth and which no book jacket can do without. It is a quality which no one can put his finger on in any exact critical sense, so it is always safe for anybody to use. Usually I think what is meant by it is that the writer excuses all human weakness because human weakness is human. The kind of hazy compassion demanded of the writer now makes it difficult to be anti-anything.[5]

Further, in her essay "Novelist and Believer"—and let me pause a moment here to say that anyone who is interested in being a writer ought to go out and buy her collection of essays *Mystery and Manners* right now—she puts her finger exactly on what the believer ought to know is the difference between hazy compassion and the making of excuses for human behavior. She writes:

> The Christian novelist is distinguished from his pagan colleagues by recognizing sin as sin. According to his heritage he sees it not as sickness or an accident of environment, but as a responsible choice of offense against God which involves his eternal future. Either one is serious about salvation or one is not.[6]

What she's saying here—actually, what she *said* nearly fifty years ago—is not one breath less true today. Compassion is the new and ultimate religion of the writer of literary fiction. Compassion is wisdom, is love, is genuine heart—all virtues none of us will disdain for fear of being accused, as Kant did of those who depended on the guidance of another, of being cowards in the face of human reason.

But I'd like to cite a different text for a moment here, one a lot older than either Flannery's or Kant's, one that speaks of the folly of such notions as the preeminence of man's reason. Get a load of this:

> For although they knew God, they did not honor him as God or give thanks to him, but they became futile in their thinking, and their foolish hearts were darkened. Claiming to be wise, they became fools. . . . Therefore God gave them up in the lusts of their hearts to impurity, to the dishonoring of their bodies among themselves, because they exchanged the truth about God for a lie and worshiped and served the creature rather than the Creator.

That's Paul, by the way, in the first chapter of Romans (vv. 21–25). Oh, and this one:

> Let no one deceive himself. If anyone among you thinks that he is wise in this age, let him become a fool that he may become wise. For the wisdom of this world is folly with God.

Paul again, in chapter 3 of 1 Corinthians (vv. 18–19).

Francis Schaeffer, in *The Great Evangelical Disaster*, comments on these passages from Paul:

> What is involved here is the way men think, the process of reasoning, thought, and comprehension. Thus "their thinking became futile and their foolish hearts were darkened. Although they claimed to be wise, they became fools." When the Scripture speaks of a man being foolish in this way, it does not mean he is only foolish religiously. Rather, it means that he has accepted a position that is intellectually foolish not only with regard to what the Bible says, but also to what exists concerning the universe and its form and what it means

> to be human. In turning away from God and the truth which
> he has given, man has thus become *foolishly* foolish in regard
> to what man is and what the universe is. Man is left with
> a position with which he cannot live, and he is caught in a
> multitude of intellectual and personal tensions.[7]

These tensions Schaeffer points out as being the logical end of a
world fooled into believing in itself as God are what we've wound
up calling *angst*, a word that, like *epiphany*, was first used in a
religious sense. Søren Kierkegaard, in reaction to Georg Hegel's
proposed universe of reason and reality as the sole and ultimately
unifying principles, employed the word *angst* to describe the anxiety
felt deep in man's heart when faced with the uncrossable chasm
between God and our broken world. But then the existentialists
took up the word in the twentieth century to stand for the feeling of
being backed into a corner, without, it seems, recognizing that it was
ourselves who were doing the backing up, until we'd hit the hard
corner behind us of our own illegitimate deification.

One need only look at the way in which these two words, *epiphany* and *angst*, have been diminished in their meaning because they
have been arrogated by a world bent on proving God doesn't exist.
Once stolen, these words moved from the shining forth of Christ
to the shining forth of man, and from the sense of fear and trembling at the approach to the throne of grace, to the sense of fear and
trembling over a purposeless and pointless life.

The thesis of G. K. Chesterton's *The Everlasting Man*, published
in 1925, is that "those who say that Christ stands side by side with
similar myths, and his religion side by side with similar religions,
are only repeating a very stale formula contradicted by a very striking fact."[8] The fact, of course, is Christ's role in history as God made
flesh, and Chesterton's book serves up beautifully and intelligently
why man's foolishly believing in the power of himself leads to the
dead end of himself, and why man's shining forth on himself leaves

us to this day with the angst we know and have come to accept as part and parcel of our lives. In it he writes:

> Certainly the pagan does not disbelieve like an atheist, any more than he believes like a Christian. He feels the presence of powers, about which he guesses and invents. St. Paul said that the Greeks had one altar to an unknown god. But in truth all their gods were unknown gods. And the real break in history did come when St. Paul declared to them whom they had ignorantly worshipped.
>
> *The substance of all such paganism may be summarized thus. It is an attempt to reach the divine reality through the imagination alone;* in its own field reason does not restrain it at all. *It is vital to the view of all history that reason is something separate from religion even in the most rational of these civilizations.* It is only as an afterthought, when such cults are decadent or on the defensive, that a few Neo-Platonists or a few Brahmins are found trying to rationalise them, and even then only by trying to allegorise them. *But in reality the rivers of mythology and philosophy run parallel and do not mingle till they reach the sea of Christendom. Simple secularists still talk as if the Church had introduced a sort of schism between reason and religion. The truth is that the Church was actually the first thing that ever tried to combine reason and religion.* There had never before been any such union of the priests and the philosophers.[9]

And so here, finally, is where *I* can begin, I believe, to talk about reclaiming literary fiction: we must see that, as with the fact of our being forgiven, *the work of reclaiming has already been accomplished.* Christ's insertion into history combined once and for all story and logic, imagination and reason. We, like those thinkers Paul warns us against, have been foolishly fooled into believing in a literary aesthetic that holds as its assumptions, its prejudiced beginning points, a schism between imagination and philosophy, between story and supernatural meaning. And we have believed as well—and again foolishly—that to believe the twain shall meet requires a kind of cowardice on our part as believers in the need for guidance from another, no matter that the Good Shepherd whose voice we recognize is that guide.

That is, if we are believers in Christ, we must recognize that we are frolicking in the sea of Christendom and not swimming upstream in either of the twin rivers of imagination or philosophy. We have been saved.

We as believers must see that there is no one save Satan who stills our fingers over a keyboard when we, with fear and trembling, begin to write of our "human attestation" to the role of grace in our lives.

But.

But, you may say.

Let's be realistic. The world of books is run, by and large, by the notions of money and how much can be made. One gatekeeper—let's just call it "New York"—is by and large uninterested in the supernatural, save in the bankability of the supernatural's demonic sense. The other gatekeeper, Christian publishing—mysteriously like its evil twin, New York—is by and large uninterested in the supernatural, save in the bankability of the supernatural's ability to comfort the already convinced. Christian publishing in this way, it seems to me—and I do not say this lightly or to condemn—is undoubtedly even more uninterested in *art* than New York, and we must admit as well that this leaves us with no other conclusion to draw than what Christian publishing is most interested in—and again mysteriously like its evil twin, New York—is how deep the pockets are of the choir to which it already preaches.

Please know, again, that I do not say this lightly, nor do I say this to lay blame for the lack of good writing that wrestles not with the contrivances of plot but with the contrivances of the human heart anywhere but at my own feet. Again, no one except Satan stills my fingers at the keyboard when it comes to my creating art that is

Christ-centered. No one. And I believe, as Christ told the Pharisees who wanted him to quiet the crowds calling out, "Blessed is the king who comes in the name of the Lord!" on his triumphant entry into Jerusalem, that if we keep quiet even the stones will cry out.

But even so, you, if you are a writer of fiction that has no genre but that *of* the human heart, have every right to ask, how do we write literary fiction that is built upon a supernatural God, in a world that doesn't want to hear it?

And you wouldn't be the first to ask that. Not by a long shot. Let me pause a moment here and quote once more a few passages from Flannery O'Connor, because this is ground she tread upon a long time ago and wrote about so very much clearer than I ever could. Here she is, in her second letter to a friend known only as "A," writing in August of 1955:

> One of the awful things about writing when you are a Christian is that for you the ultimate reality is the Incarnation, the present reality is the Incarnation, and nobody believes in the Incarnation; that is, nobody in your audience. My audience are the people who think God is dead. At least these are the people I am conscious of writing for.[10]

And this, again from the essay "Novelist and Believer":

> It makes a great deal of difference to the look of a novel whether its author believes that the world came late into being and continues to come by a creative act of God, or whether he believes that the world and ourselves are the product of a cosmic accident. It makes a great difference to his novel whether he believes that we are created in God's image, or whether he believes we create God in our own. It makes a great difference whether he believes that our wills are free, or bound like those of the other animals.[11]

And this bright indictment of us all, true and true and true:

Ever since there have been such things as novels, the world has been flooded with bad fiction for which the religious impulse has been responsible. The sorry religious novel comes about when the writer supposes that because of his belief, he is somehow dispensed from the obligation to penetrate concrete reality. He will think that the eyes of the Church or of the Bible or of his particular theology have already done the seeing for him, and that his business is to rearrange this essential vision into satisfying patterns, getting himself as little dirty as possible.[12]

And finally this, from the essay "Catholic Novelists and Their Readers," a passage that brings us, ultimately, right back to this notion of marketplace, and of value:

St. Thomas Aquinas says that art does not require rectitude of the appetite, that it is wholly concerned with the good of that which is made. He says that a work of art is a good in itself, and this is a truth that the modern world has largely forgotten. We are not content to stay within our limitations and make something that is simply a good in and by itself. Now we want to make something that will have some utilitarian value. Yet what is good in itself glorifies God because it reflects God. The artist has his hands full and does his duty if he attends to his art. He can safely leave evangelizing to the evangelists. He must first of all be aware of his limitations as an artist—for art transcends its limitations only by staying within them.[13]

It seems to me that if we look either to Christian publishing or to New York for our venue, for our outlet, for our *income*, as it were, from writing about the human being in relation to a supernatural God, then we have missed the point of creating in God's name entirely. If we are asking why have we given up the ghost for any reason other than a desire to better serve God, then we are no better—I mean this—than the silversmiths under Demetrius at Ephesus, craftsmen who were more interested in the income off their silver shrines to and images of Artemis than they were in the good news Paul proclaimed.

But allow me, if you will, one last faith story. One last story of our supernatural God.

I was born again after a Josh McDowell rally when I was eighteen. Then, by hook and by crook, I ended up in a creative-writing classroom for no good reason other than that it was an elective. I had a good time, though I'd never in my life thought of being a writer. The thought never crossed my mind.

A couple of years later, a newlywed getting ready to head off with my wife to study writing at grad school in Massachusetts, I decided to begin sending out my stories for publication.

I bought a little plastic file box in order to keep my rejections— the ones I knew would be on their way—and to house as well my own filing system of what I had sent where.

But before I sent out my first story, I sat down at the small table we had in our apartment in Long Beach, California, and wrote out this verse, and then prayed it:

Commit your work to the LORD,
and your plans will be established. (Prov. 16:3)

I have the piece of paper right here; I can still see the remnants of the yellowed Scotch tape I used to tape it to the inside lid of that filing box. To this day I keep this scrap, written in my twenty-one-year-old hand, taped to the wall above my desk.

I now have in my box of rejections 601 of them; I have kept all but one (that's another story) since that day in 1980. This does not count the number of rejections of my novels and story collections; as best as I can tell, there are perhaps forty of those.

But also to this day, before I begin writing—and most certainly before I began writing out this essay both for you and for me—I commit, in prayer, my works to the Lord, so that my plans will be established.

Letters

What I continue to learn through my life as a writer—through all those rejections and successes, past, present, and yet to come—is that the plan I want established is not to succeed in the world's terms but in God's terms. The loving God who loves us on his terms, and his only.

I continue to learn to relinquish my plans for success and simply plan to do, as clearly as the Holy Spirit leads me, God's will, and not my own.

And here I am, the writer I have become because of the supernatural intervention in my life of a loving God—the *only* true God. Certainly not an answer to prayer as quick as that given when, on a hot summer day on a playground in Moldova, we called out for gum, and certainly not as mysteriously achieved as the appearing of the right number of T-shirts for kids who had just heard the good news of Jesus Christ.

But supernatural all the same, that I would be given the blessing of being able to write all this down, over thirty years after I'd scrawled Proverbs 16:3 on this piece of paper.

Which leads to the end of my long-winded beginning of this book.

I want to ask in closing, do you believe in a supernatural God?

Do you believe in a God who provides, in love, T-shirts and loaves of bread? In gum and oddball phone calls and the atoning work of a son he gave to die for us?

Do you believe that the rocks will cry out if we, with our art, don't cry out, "Blessed is the King who comes in the name of the Lord"?

And if you do, I have to ask, then how can you write with any eye whatsoever on the foolishness of a world that tells you that the truth, rather than setting you free, has caged you in its self-induced and pointless angst, and that the shining forth of Christ is a myth, to be replaced by the feeble shining forth of man on himself?

For whom do you write?

And are you willing?

The Artist and the City, or, Some Random Thoughts on Why We Are Here

As a Christian who writes books for a world wider than the community in which he operates daily, I have to say I've had to reckon with two questions over these many years I've been at work: (1) What is the relationship between the believing artist and the public square? and (2) How might the artist's quest to understand what it means to be human influence the way church and society address one another?

These are big questions, I know. And now that I am writing this thing out, I find that it seems there is a heck of a lot more to say about this topic than I can possibly address here. Really. The idea of being a believing artist *and* a citizen touches on every conceivable aspect of one's life, if you let yourself see this way of being—this being an artist—as truly *a way of being.*

Cardinal Henri-Marie de Lubac, the French Roman Catholic integral to the Second Vatican Council, wrote, "Truth is not a good that I possess. . . . It is such that in giving it I must still receive it; in discovering it I still have to search for it."[1] This giving away the truth we are given is a good place to start when we begin to think about what roles we are to have as artists in the community in which we live. That is, because we are blessed, we don't keep it. Rather, we are to be blessings to others; we are blessed to be a blessing (at least I think that's what de Lubac might at least be touching upon).

One other point from the Second Vatican Council (as if there weren't plenty otherwise) was the Inter Mirifica of December 4, 1963, the Decree on the Means of Social Communication, which addressed the relation of the media and society, point six of which regards "the relation between the rights of art . . . and the moral law," and which holds, rightly, I believe, that "all must accept the absolute primacy of the objective moral order," and that that order alone "is superior to and is capable of harmonizing all forms of human activity, not excepting art, no matter how noble in themselves."[2]

So if we are, first as believers, blessed to be a blessing, and next as artists, blessed to be a blessing (because that is who I am going to assume is reading what I'm penning this moment: believers pursuing the creation of art), then we necessarily have a relationship to the moral order our creator God has imposed upon us. Here is our truest beginning point of an understanding of the creation of art by the Christian: the created world has a moral order to which we must submit, and through that submission and only through that submission will harmony and beauty and truth even begin to be approached by us who profess to practice art. Further, we do not commit art in a vacuum but are a part of society—of humanity—at large, and therefore we indeed have a role in that society, a role that can and will contribute to the harmonization of human activity at large. We have been blessed to be a blessing.

Art as practiced by believers began as an act of harmony between God and man. The best and first example I know of not to *illustrate* this founding principle but to *be* this founding principle is one of my favorite people in the Bible: none other than our old pal Bezalel, that man named by God in Exodus 31 to be the one to craft the tabernacle, the ark, and all the instruments of worship God has planned for the nation of Israel while it wanders there in the desert all those years and until first David and then Solomon get their dispatches from the same and only God as to how the temple itself will be built.

Exodus 31 begins, "Then the LORD spoke to Moses, saying: 'See, I have called by name Bezalel the son of Uri, the son of Hur, of the tribe of Judah. And I have filled him with the Spirit of God, in wisdom, in understanding, in knowledge, and in all *manner of* workmanship, to design artistic works, to work in gold, in silver, in bronze, in cutting jewels for setting, in carving wood, and to work in all manner of workmanship'" (vv. 1–5 NKJV).

This is one of my favorite passages. Really. Here is a man *named* by God, picked out of the entire displaced nation, because of the gift from God of his artistry. Imagine that: being named by God, right there in his words for all time and eternity, as being the artist who will create what God has in mind for worship. What I find so awesome—and I mean that word in its truest sense—is that Bezalel appears only in Exodus 31 and then again in chapters 35 through 38 only because he is an artist. He is no relation to Aaron but is of the tribe of Judah (and therefore of the tribe of Christ, but that will be hundreds of years later), and so will have no role in the administering of the sacrifices that will take place in what he will have created. As a member of the tribe of Judah he's not even one of the Levite clans—Gershon, Kohath, and Merari—whose honor it will be to wrap up and tote all those exquisite items he will have made from one desert outpost to the next. Because of the holiness of what he has created, Bezalel won't even be allowed to *see* what he has been called by God to create once it has been assembled and Moses is allowed to enter the Most Holy Place.

But create he does, along with his second in command, another artist named by God a little later on, Aholiab. The two of them were called to create, along with "every gifted artisan in whom the LORD has put wisdom and understanding" (36:1 NKJV), what God desires them to create. There's the ark of the covenant, and the candlestick, and the altar of burnt offering, and the laver and all the utensils to be used, as well as the hangings that will encompass the holy court, and the screen for the court that would separate it from the Holy Place, and the veil, of course, that would separate the Holy Place from the Most Holy Place, where the ark itself would reside—all of it made with the best materials around, from gold and silver and bronze to acacia wood and jewels, the finest linen possible, and the blue and purple and scarlet thread. Not to mention all those badger skins to cover everything.

All this craftsmanship, all this artistry, all this *creativity*, accomplished by hands blessed by God to accomplish this creation; indeed, Bezalel and the other artists were blessed to be a blessing in order to create for God what was at that time the center of his glory. The tabernacle, this mobile temple from which God's moral order emanated in the form of the laws handed down to Moses, and this conduit through which man's sacrifices made in thanks to God's mercy and by his command were sent up to heaven, that "sweet aroma, an offering made by fire to the LORD" (Ex. 29:18 NKJV), was built through individual artists working in harmony with God's direction (and as an aside here, please note: the role of harmony is assigned to us created beings; the melody is our creator God's moral order, which will never change, and which, in musical terms, is never out of tune; dissonance between melody and harmony occurs only when the harmonic line wanders off one way or the other).

And as a further aside, and to show you how much a rube I really am, my wife and I lived in Jerusalem from the fall of 2006 to the spring of 2007, where I served as a Fulbright senior American scholar and writer in residence at Bar Ilan University in Tel Aviv. While living in Jerusalem we made friends with a good number of people, worshiping at the Baptist Center with a small band of believers from around the world. While there I also made the acquaintance of a young couple, both of them writers, who were completed Jews. We were having lunch one day at a bookstore/restaurant, the

name of which I won't even begin to try to pronounce here, and at
one point I started in on my hero, Bezalel, and told them who he
was and why he was important and how wonderful it was that the
artist had been named by God—all that.

All this time I was noticing the strange sort of looks on their
faces, the glances they were exchanging, the small nervous smiles
and nods they were giving me as I went on and on until I stopped,
then said, "You guys have heard of Bezalel, right?" because I thought
perhaps I'd gone too biblically deep for them, or at least had mispro-
nounced his name, something along those lines.

That was when the woman—and God bless her for her patience
with me, and her care and tact and love in Christ—nodded and
smiled, said, "Yes. There's, umm, actually a university named after
him here."

And the man said, "Bezalel Academy of Arts and Design," and
pointed his thumb over his shoulder in the general direction. "Over
on Bezalel Street."

Turns out this is the national arts university of Israel, and I'd
walked or driven past it fifty times at least. Turns out, too, that it
was one of the first institutes of learning set in motion as part of
Theodor Herzl's plan for a return of the Jewish people to create a
nation in Palestine and that the institute itself began in 1906 there
in Jerusalem.

And here I was, Mr. Fulbright senior American scholar, purport-
ing to teach them about a man they had obviously known since pre-
school and after whom the nation of Israel built its arts university.

What a rube.

But the importance of Bezalel, *and so to understanding our role
as artists under God*, cannot be underestimated: under his watch
were created sculpture, tapestry, woodcarving, jewelry, clothing,
metalwork, even architecture, and all of it done without signing
a name to a single piece of it, all of it done knowing full well he
wouldn't even be allowed to participate in its use once he and all

the artists involved completed their creations, *and all of it done in creation of the public square itself*, this place where God was to be worshiped and from which his order issued.

Once they were finished, their only participation would be as members of the nation of Israel, gathered in the public square before the tabernacle; their only participation would be their role as citizens who, "when Moses went and told the people all the LORD's words and laws . . . responded with one voice, 'Everything the LORD has said we will do'" (Ex. 24:3 NIV).

The role of the artist? Creator in a worship relationship to God; citizen in a worship relationship to God.

But things don't work like that anymore.

With Christ's death and resurrection, the idea of a temple in which God resides has been done away with; Christ lives in me. The public square is now, here in the United States, our democracy, and a place in which all religions are tolerated, and this is good and right, if our country is to be a democracy. Folks who continue to say—and oftentimes it seems they are the evangelicals among us— that our country was founded by Christians are wrong, and to call "Christians" important, even integral people to the establishment of our country, such as Thomas Jefferson and Benjamin Franklin, is to sorely miss the facts of their lives. And though the creation of art for God's sake has continued to one degree and another and in one form and another from Bezalel's day to this, art's necessity to the public square—that is, the need for that harmony created by artists working within God's moral order to be witnessed by citizens united in their faith in the one true God—simply isn't the world in which we live. Art for God's sake has waned significantly for many a reason, but chiefly and at core because Satan, who is real, has done his utmost to convince us all, believer and nonbeliever alike, to divorce art from God.

The following is a quote from an essay titled "The Dilemma of

Filmmaking" by the late Ingmar Bergman, one of the supreme film artists—one of the supreme *artists*—of the twentieth century. Mr. Bergman was raised in a devoutly religious family, though as far as we can know from this side of heaven, he was not a believer. But the following observation about contemporary art and its relationship to God—made in 1954 when Bergman was only forty-six years old and so not an old man looking ruefully back on his life (*The Seventh Seal* was still three years away!), is startlingly true:

> Regardless of my own beliefs and my own doubts, which are completely without importance in this connection, it is my opinion that art lost its creative urge the moment it was separated from worship. It severed the umbilical cord and lives its own sterile life, generating and degenerating itself. The individual has become the highest form and greatest bane of artistic creation. Creative unity and humble anonymity are forgotten and buried relics without significance or meaning. The smallest cuts and moral pains of the ego are examined under the microscope as if they were of eternal importance.[3]

Here Bergman puts his finger on the exact pulse point of why art for God's sake no longer matters: man, as he has been doing since the garden (more on that anon), placed himself on the throne of meaning and purpose; and art, man's creation intended to be produced in harmony with God, wandered away. The result, as Bergman points out, is an utter preoccupation with the self; the result is an unmoored harmonic line, consumed with believing itself the melody.

Further, as regards art being cut loose from God's moral order—his worship—I'm going to quote (and will again in a little while) from a brilliant book every artist ought to own and memorize. I know I am risking being that fool at the table in a bookstore/restaurant in Jerusalem carrying on as though I had discovered Bezalel to an audience for whom the name was common knowledge; maybe most readers of this essay already have this book, or read it thirty-five years ago when it came out, or are on their seventh copy, so thumb-worn and underlined became the pages of the prior six, but here goes: *Art and the Bible*, by Francis Schaeffer. Yes, that old Hobbit-like fellow in the knickers and sporting the funky little white beard.

Art and the Bible is a wondrous and necessary book for anyone seeking to know, as Schaeffer writes in the first line of the book, "What is the role of art in the Christian life?" Written in the early seventies during the Jesus Movement, the book sought to calm down a lot of people who were worried about all this strange new Christian stuff going down, especially this new music and its intrusion into the old church. But the book doesn't focus on music; it addresses not only the history of art and the church but also standards for what art ought to be and how artists ought to think of themselves in an age when the worldly artist was given (and continues to be given) carte blanche when it comes to moral order. Here's the quote:

> The notion of Bohemian freedom which Jean Jacques Rousseau promulgated and which has been so prevalent in modern society has no place in Christian thinking. Rousseau was seeking a kind of autonomous freedom, and from him stemmed a group of "supermen" whose lives were lived above reason, as it were, and above the norms of society. For a long time this Bohemian life was taken to be the ideal for the artist, and it has come in the last few decades to be considered an ideal for more than the artist. From a Christian point of view, however, this sort of life is not allowed. God's Word binds the great man and the small, the king and the artist.[4]

Good ole Francis Schaeffer. He called 'em like he saw 'em. How many of us who claim to be artists or at least want to be called such—and be honest now, as God is our witness—have done so in one form or another, to excuse our being lazy, or forgetful, or just plain irresponsible?

Rousseau, of course, would be proud of the number of us who have, while Schaefer would have put his hand to his white-haired chin, and slowly shaken his head.

The fact is that this sort of giving oneself a pass on being responsible because one is an artist, to whatever degree we give ourselves that right, is to embrace the Rousseauian notion of what an artist is: one who is not held back by any moral order. And so how is it that we who proclaim Christ suppose that we can create art that will be in harmony with the moral order imposed by the God who has called us to create?

Please understand that I know— boy, do I know—that art stems oftentimes from the broken, that true and deep and meaningful creation can and often does find its being through shattered lives. John Gardner in *On Becoming a Novelist* writes in what sounds like a rather cavalier fashion, "A psychological wound is helpful, if it can be kept in partial control, to keep the novelist driven. Some fatal childhood accident for which one feels responsible and can never fully forgive oneself; a sense that one never quite earned one's parents' love; shame about one's origins—belligerent defensive guilt about one's race or country upbringing or the physical handicaps of one's parents—or embarrassment about one's own physical appearance: all these are promising signs."[5]

And though, as I said, Gardner, the author most famously of *Grendel* as well as such fine novels as *The Sunlight Dialogs* and *October Light*, sounds rather cavalier here, in fact downright cold-blooded about wounds that help the artist, it is interesting to note that his most famous short story, *Redemption*, begins with a boy named Jack Hawthorne accidentally running over and killing his little brother with a cultipacker and tells the story of his ongoing search for redemption in the face of his assumed guilt.[6] And when one finds out that, in fact, Gardner ran over and killed his little brother with a cultipacker when he was a boy, his assertion here that a wound—that is, *a continued search for healing through that wound*—can help the artist create art earns him a level of gravitas we might not otherwise be so willing to give him.

All of which is to say that the art I am here speaking of that is to be in harmony with our creator God's moral order does not mean art that is necessarily happy; it does not mean art that cheers us up and puts a sunny smile on our faces. Nor does it mean that the creators of that art must be slaphappy folks just makin' art for the Lord. No. No. And one more time: No.

Schaeffer, in *Art and the Bible*, breaks Christian art into what he calls *minor* and *major* themes. The former regards the "abnormality of the revolting world"; the latter, art that regards the "meaningfulness and purposefulness of life." He writes:

> Christian art needs to recognize the minor theme, the defeated aspect to even the Christian life. If our Christian art only emphasizes the major theme, then it is not fully Christian but simply romantic art. . . . Older Christians may wonder what is wrong with this art and wonder why their kids are turned off by it, but the answer is simple. It's romantic. It's based on the notion that Christianity has only an optimistic note.
>
> On the other hand, it is possible for a Christian to so major on the minor theme, emphasizing the lostness of man and the abnormality of the universe, that he is equally unbiblical.[7]

I can see ole Francis chuckling at his little pun there, majoring on the minor theme, but his assertion is absolutely true: art in harmony with our creator God is art that must encompass the whole of man's experience, its depravity and triumph both.

Creating in harmony with God does not call for the art to be necessarily upright and pleasing, nor does it call for the artist to be healed and happy. But in this day, when we as believing artists have largely been cut off from the sort of role Bezalel and company were blessed to have lived and now live in a day and age when the artist no longer creates in anonymous humility but has been crowned with many crowns and is not expected to show up on time, and when his art seeks at worst to rub our noses in the stained carpet of his beliefs about us all, and at best seeks to show us the glory we have earned for ourselves, we as believers seeking harmony with God's order must create with a redemptive view of man. We no longer create for a movable tabernacle but for the completed temple our individual beings can be: that place in which Christ resides until we reside with him in eternity. We must now create, in both minor and major modes, portraits of humanity that extend to all who have ears to hear and eyes to see the value of humanity for our having been created by God in his image. Because if we don't, what other portrait do we have to bring to our God but the pointlessness of his creation?

Finally, any examination of the question of the responsibility the believing artist has to the city—to the culture at large—must acknowledge that the story of the Bible is *not* one of corporate actions but of individual relationships of the created with the Creator. Creation in his name and to his honor and glory began with a whisper to a man named Abram who then set out into the desert to create for his God the nation that God called him to create. This whisper to create continued through the nation of Israel to Moses, then to Joshua, the prophets, and to Christ, of course, and to Paul and the disciples. The entire Bible is made up of individual people acting—that is, creating—either in their own names and to their own glory or in God's name and to his glory. This has been so since the creation of man, since the moment when God, in his purpose and glory, spoke into being—spoke into *creation*—this world, and all of us here. As a refresher, here is Genesis 3:1–5 (NKJV):

> Now the serpent was more cunning than any beast of the field which the LORD God had made. And he said to the woman, "Has God indeed said, 'You shall not eat of every tree of the garden'?" And the woman said to the serpent, "We may eat the fruit of the trees of the garden; but of the fruit of the

tree which *is* in the midst of the garden, God has said, 'You shall not eat it, nor shall you touch it, lest you die.'" Then the serpent said to the woman, "You will not surely die. For God knows that in the day you eat of it your eyes will be opened, and you will be like God, knowing good and evil."

Satan's entry into the world God created and his first creation—*his first, last, and only attempt at creating a work of art*—is the lie all of us have found so attractive and have embraced since before we were cognizant beings. It is the lie we have not only believed but also inherited, the stain Adam left upon us all; it is the lie from which we must flee if we are to be reunited in and through and by Christ with our Creator, and if we have any hope at all of having a role in our society. Satan's attempt at art, an abject failure because, finally and gloriously, of the work of pure and perfect and wholly whole art—Christ on the cross—was the destruction of the beautiful relationship between our creator God and us his created beings; it was to get us to believe God to be a liar and to get ourselves to believe in ourselves. It was to get us to believe that our harmonic line was more valuable than the melody that will forever remain true.

Satan failed, and next to the perfect work of art that is Christ's work on the cross is the life of the believer lived out in belief; it is the life of the created lived out in thankfulness and in humility and in service—in *creation*—to our creator God. Our relationship to the public square is to live in full acknowledgment of who our Creator is; the public square, which like us all is and will remain fallen, will make of us what God wills.

You have heard from me no words about what we ought to do tomorrow to effect change in the public square through our roles as believing artists. You have read here no reports from Washington, where I serve on the National Council on the Arts, a committee that oversees the National Endowment for the Arts to make sure the money you pay in taxes that the government sets aside for the arts is spent wisely. And you have heard from me no call to political action, or to proselytizing, or to wearing wristbands with the initials *WWJW*—"What would Jesus write?"

I know who I am is our relationship to the public square, and because of who we are—creations of the one true creator God—my only call to you as artists striving to create in harmony with God's order is to create, and to do so in order to live lives that are blessings themselves.

"Truth is not a good that I possess," wrote Cardinal de Lubac. "It is such that in giving it I must still receive it; in discovering it I still have to search for it."[8]

On Precision

Here's a quote I keep taped to the wall above my desk, which is to say it is an important one, one of my favorites, and one that helps me when I write. It's from a memoir piece the poet Phil Levine wrote that appeared in the journal *Ploughshares* a few years ago. It's about his having been a student in one of those legendary workshops at Iowa, this one taught by none other than John Berryman, that madman prophet whose lips were touched by the searing coal of poetry. Levine writes that one day Berryman gave the assembled young writers the following monumentally inspiring and intensely intimidating exhortation: "You should always be trying to write a poem you are unable to write, a poem you lack the technique, the language, the courage to achieve. Otherwise, you're merely imitating yourself, going nowhere because that's always easiest."[1] When one considers that the students sitting in that classroom—those snot-nosed kids waiting to start their own lives as poets—included not only Levine but also W. D. Snodgrass, Donald Justice, Robert Dana, Constance Urdang, Jane Cooper, Henri Coulette, and William Stafford, it's easy to see the effect of taking such a difficult piece of wisdom to heart.

I give that quote to you in an effort to do a little throat clearing, a little stretching and knuckle cracking before I get on to what I want to write about, because although I am going to do my best, I do not believe that I can even begin to tell you how important the subject of this essay is to good writing. And by good writing, I mean writing that will last, and that will mean something, and that will have pierced the heart and soul and mind not only of our readers but, more importantly, of ourselves. Precision is *the* most important element to crafting a piece of prose—and to crafting a poem, in fact, to crafting *any* piece of writing, from an obituary to a grocery list to the name you give a new file on your computer.

I have wanted for years to write about this particular element of writing because, time and time and time again, I have seen in my students' work its certain lack. And yet I *haven't* written about it through all these years because the notion of actually doing so seems overwhelming; the subject concerns, well, pretty much everything there is to say about writing: *you must be precise.* How would I even begin, I have often thought, to wrestle down precision in writing to a topic that could be encompassed by words, and not just words at large but by my *own* pitiful store of them?

How, precisely, can I do this?

But it is precisely (ahem) this inability to address the subject and precisely my desire to address it nonetheless that spurs me on in putting together this essay; it is precisely my lack of language, technique, and courage to write this out that makes me write it out.

I am the one, it turns out, who wants to know why precision is the most important element to writing, and the only way for me to encounter its importance is to try to write about that importance.

Why all this hubbub about precision? you may ask. Isn't it just about finding the right word for the moment at hand, about giving good details to your writing so that it will be vivid and memorable? Isn't precision of thought just about being focused in on what you really *mean* when you are writing and putting clearly into words what your characters are seeing and feeling and thinking?

Of course, and in the abstract world of such questions, this all looks quite easy and accomplishable. The noun *precision* is only, after all, the "quality, condition, or fact of being exact and accurate," to quote the Oxford American Dictionary; further, the adjective *pre-*

cise is the quality of being "marked by exactness and accuracy of expression or detail." Fair enough.

But as a teacher of writing, my simply saying that writing must be precise and that precision is only about using the right word at the right moment is somewhat akin to pulling up to the auto mechanic's shop, your car's engine rattling in its last death gasps, and asking the mechanic if he knows what's wrong. Carefully he lifts up the hood, leans over the shuddering wreck of an engine, then takes a rag from his back pocket, rubs his hands together. "Here's your problem," he says, and stands, turns to you, waiting there in dumb anticipation. Sagely he nods at you, then says, "Your engine's broke."

We must be precise about what we mean when we say "precise."

In *The Art of Fiction* John Gardner writes the following on the complexity of finding the way to give a story the precision its life requires:

> He must think out completely, as coolly as any critic, what his fiction means, or is trying to mean. He must complete his equations, think out the subtlest implications of what he's said, get at the truth not just of his characters and action but also of his fiction's form, remembering that neatness can be carried too far, so that the work begins to seem fussy and overwrought, anal compulsive, unspontaneous, and remembering that, on the other hand, mess is no adequate alternative. He must think as cleanly as a mathematician, but he must also know by intuition when to sacrifice precision for some higher good, how to simplify, take short cuts, keep the foreground up there in front and the background back.[2]

The sort of precision I mean to talk about is the ineffable kind, the kind that comes from the intuition Gardner talks about, the sort of accuracy that reaches beyond your knowing what you mean. The kind of accuracy I am talking about here is that for which you don't have the language, and for which perhaps you don't have the technique, and for which you don't have the courage to find.

Letters

Courage is an old-fashioned word, and I am sure I am not alone when I say that when I hear that word, I oftentimes think of the cowardly lion in *The Wizard of Oz*, Bert Lahr done up in that crazy costume replete with a tail that has a mind of its own. "Courage!" he calls for in his strangely Brooklyn accent, though he is ostensibly a Kansas field hand in his life on earth.

But it is a good word, one we need to get out and dust off now and again to remind us that every word you write down is *your* assertion and insertion into a world of both thought and image that hasn't existed until you wrote down that word. Yet simply writing down words isn't in and of itself a courageous act; it only becomes so when the words and the order in which you laced them aren't borrowed from the vast steaming pile of clichés we always have ready at hand. Gardner, this time in *On Becoming a Novelist*, writes,

> The writer with the worst odds—the person to whom one at once says, "I don't think so"—is the writer whose feel for language seems incorrigibly perverted. The most obvious example is the writer who cannot move without the help of such phrases as "with a merry twinkle in her eye," or "the adorable twins," or "his hearty, booming laugh"—dead expressions, the cranked-up zombie emotion of a writer who feels nothing in his daily life or *nothing he trusts enough to find his own words for*, so that he turns instead to "she stifled a sob," "friendly lopsided smile," "cocking an eyebrow in that quizzical way he had," "his broad shoulders," "his encircling arm," "a faint smile curving her lips," "his voice was husky," "her face framed by auburn curls."[3]

Courage is necessary to setting aside these sorts of phrases so that we can find our own, trusting somehow that those precise words we don't yet know will serve the purpose of showing us what we can't yet see.

And just as words themselves can betray us by their overuse—paradoxically, an overuse that has been precipitated by their actually having worked before, because clichés spring from having been the perfect description at some point in the past—so can scenes and characters and even stories themselves—of course even stories themselves!—be solely clichés because we do not have the courage to plumb the depths of our own experience.

I once taught at a writers' conference at which one of the students turned in a story about a homeless person. The story was big-hearted and generous and showed plenty of compassion—and rang absolutely false. In it a homeless man lives in a cardboard box in a small community of cardboard box dwellers in a back alley. In it the homeless man has a heart of gold, and his being a homeless person stems from his being misunderstood by both his family and society. His homies (or homelessies?) are all kind and quirky and say the darndest things. His downfall, finally, and why he can't ever fit into society is revealed to be that he simply doesn't fit in.

When I read a story like this, one that has by all indications absolutely no foundation in any sort of reality—that is, the story consisted of one cliché piled upon another and another and another—my reaction is to want to ask the author a point-blank, intrusive, and, well, presumptuous question: what exact moment out of the author's life—what genuine single true experience—happened such that the false story at hand was the result? What happened, I want to know, that made you turn from *that* to *this*?

It is a dangerous question. I don't ask it very often. I believe wholly in the free will of the author and so in the author's right to write about anything he or she pleases. Perhaps the question itself is simply a selfish one; because I have just been handed a story that does not let me experience any truth, either capital T or otherwise, I want to get my money's worth and hear what really happened. One of my credos is a quote from the American photographer Walker Evans, a quote I think so highly of that I used it as the epigraph to my own book on writing. "Stare," Evans wrote. "It is the way to educate your eye, and more. Stare, pry, listen, eavesdrop. Die knowing something. You are not here long."[4]

Letters

But whether it is due to a desire for truth or just the eavesdropper in me, I will ask the question anyway, because I believe that when something we have seen or done or felt or been told—whatever we have *experienced*—strikes us in such a way that we want to turn to an expressive form to try to create after it, there has to have been something inside that original moment worthy of our imaginations, worthy of that snagging of our creative impulse. I believe there has to have been some *there* there that makes us turn to an act of creation after having experienced that moment.

So I asked the author of this story about a homeless man—a smiling woman with wire-frame glasses who I would have regarded as middle-aged back then, though now that I think about it she was probably younger than I am now, me smack in the middle of middle age—my question, there in a workshop at a conference in a city in a state where I knew absolutely no one. I asked her the most presumptuous question you can ask someone, asked it of a stranger in the midst of a room full of strangers (for not only were there sitting at the table the eight or ten other workshop attendees, but around us all sat a good number of other people who had come to watch this part of the conference; all sessions were open to the public). I asked my question carefully, couched it and coddled it with all the respect and tact and good will I know to give, making certain as well that the author understood she didn't have to answer the question if she didn't want to.

I probably spent too many words setting it all up, too, because when finally I swallowed hard and delivered it—"What moment out of your life," I asked her, "made you think to write a story about homeless people?"—she didn't hesitate a moment, and said, "Oh, that's easy!" She then sat up a little taller in her seat and immediately went into a story about how her husband had been in the foreign service in London back then and how they had lived in a *flat*—a word she used with a kind of confident glee for how nearly exotic the word was—they had lived in a *flat*, and out front of their building had been a bus stop at which lived a homeless woman with all her belongings so that you couldn't sit on the bench while you waited for the bus.

"And the strange thing about her was that she always had this hubcap with her," the woman said, "and she was always holding it up to her chest with both hands like she was protecting it."

You would think I would have stopped her at this point for the simple fact of this hubcap showing up in the middle of things, not to mention the foreign service and London, but I didn't—I couldn't—because she was hot after telling this story she'd lived through, and she went right on without a pause to tell of the neighbor of hers who lived in the *flat* on the floor right above her own *flat* who took pity on the poor woman living out at that bus stop, and who one day brought the homeless woman upstairs to her *flat* to feed her a hot lunch of soup.

"And once my neighbor upstairs got her inside her *flat*," she said, bright and certain, "the homeless woman proceeded to break every dish in the whole place, just throwing them one by one on the floor and . . ."

"WHOA!" I shouted, then said just as loud, "STOP!" and the room was silent for a moment for how loud I'd been and how I'd cut her off.

"She really did that," the woman said then, on her face a kind of puzzled look that showed she thought somehow I might not believe her. "She really broke every dish . . ."

"No!" I nearly shouted again. "I believe you!" I said, and everyone there in the room was suddenly looking at me, wondering what was up with these loud words at the poor woman who'd just told such a great story. "What I mean is," I said, and smiled and nodded, trying not to scare them all off, chief among them this woman, "What I mean is, why didn't you tell *that* story instead of this one, about this homeless guy with a heart of gold and all these homeless people saying the darndest things?"

I really said that.

"Oh," the woman said. She shrugged, tilted her head a little and looked down at the table. "People don't want to know what happened to me."

At which everyone at the table started in on her about what a great story that was, and that she ought to write that one, and that she had to use the hubcap, and the dishes, and the bus stop, and and and . . .

My point in including this as part of an essay on how important precision is to writing? This woman, in telling the story to us, knew intuitively the value of a hubcap to her tale, and of the word *flat*, and of a broken dish, *but because she believed the precise story she herself knew had no value, she traded in that experience for a vague and clichéd and indistinguishable story it took no courage to tell.*

Precision starts with life. Precision starts with the real. Precision starts in the experiences you yourself have had, and if you want to write—and this is the crux of the whole thing—*you better pay attention to what is happening around YOU as a means by which to begin to be precise.* You better begin to look, and to see.

You better have ears to hear, and eyes to see.

Here is another example of what I mean when I am talking about precision, and I draw it from the pristine source of precision, that place the world generally believes is irrelevant and antiquated, its notions archaic and (I love the precision of this next phrase), *beside the point.* I'm talking, of course, about the Bible.

This is from the book of Judges, that wild child of a thrill ride from the Old Testament in which all hell breaks lose again and again and again, and which ends with perhaps the most rueful and forlorn words ever penned: "In those days there was no king in Israel. Everyone did what was right in his own eyes" (21:25). Judges 3:12–26 reads as follows:

> And the people of Israel again did what was evil in the sight of the LORD, and the LORD strengthened Eglon the king of Moab against Israel, because they had done what was evil in

the sight of the LORD. He gathered to himself the Ammonites and the Amalekites, and went and defeated Israel. And they took possession of the city of palms. And the people of Israel served Eglon the king of Moab eighteen years. Then the people of Israel cried out to the LORD, and the LORD raised up for them a deliverer, Ehud, the son of Gera, the Benjaminite, a left-handed man. The people of Israel sent tribute by him to Eglon the king of Moab. And Ehud made for himself a sword with two edges, a cubit in length, and he bound it on his right thigh under his clothes. And he presented the tribute to Eglon king of Moab. Now Eglon was a very fat man. And when Ehud had finished presenting the tribute, he sent away the people who carried the tribute. But he himself turned back at the idols near Gilgal and said, "I have a secret message for you, O king." And he commanded, "Silence." And all his attendants went out from his presence. And Ehud came to him as he was sitting alone in his cool roof chamber. And Ehud said, "I have a message from God for you." And he arose from his seat. And Ehud reached with his left hand, took the sword from his right thigh, and thrust it into his belly. And the hilt also went in after the blade, and the fat closed over the blade, for he did not pull the sword out of his belly; and the dung came out. Then Ehud went out into the porch and closed the doors of the roof chamber behind him and locked them. When he had gone, the servants came, and when they saw that the doors of the roof chamber were locked, they thought, "Surely he is relieving himself in the closet of the cool chamber." And they waited till they were embarrassed. But when he still did not open the doors of the roof chamber, they took the key and opened them, and there lay their lord dead on the floor. Ehud escaped while they delayed, and he passed beyond the idols and escaped to Seirah.

I have chosen this passage precisely (there's that word again) for what we probably find a bit disgusting about the whole thing and also for what we may find just a little bit amusing: first is the vivid fact of that sword of Ehud's going all the way in to Eglon's fat belly, its handle swallowed whole by his royal corpulence; and next comes the sort of comic image of these two guards standing outside the king's chamber, smelling what they do—remember that Eglon's "dung" came out—and reasoning between themselves that the king must be in his chambers and relieving himself, until they become so embarrassed and anxious over how long he has been in there that they take matters into their own hands.

When one considers that this chapter out of Israel's history was first recorded orally, handed down generation to who knows how many generations before finally being penned in Hebrew, and then weathering as many centuries as it did until first Jerome and then the scribes of King James's court copied it all out and made it new yet again, one cannot help but be amazed at the continuing immediacy, indeed the vibrant life, such concrete details retain. There's how fat the king is to these two guards glancing nervously at each other now and again to see who will risk interrupting the king on his throne, as it were, to make sure he's okay, and the fact Ehud was left-handed (as Benjaminites were), which meant the hand most likely to heft a weapon, his right, was empty, and so remained above suspicion, allowing the surprise of his left hand drawing out from his right thigh that sword.

This is what I am talking about when I say precision is the key to all good writing: giving your readers the telling detail that, because of its startling specificity, makes an occurrence thousands of years ago seem as new as this moment we are living through right now.

At the beginning of every semester, I read out loud Richard Brautigan's short story "1/3, 1/3, 1/3" to my students.[5] I do this because (1) it's a terrific story; (2) when it comes to learning craft, I place a whole lot more stock in examining well-written work than in yammering on about the *how-to* of technique; and (3) this story has two of the best descriptive sentences I have ever read.

Brautigan's writing is funny, beautiful, and strange. He was most famous for his novel *Trout Fishing in America*, published in 1967, for which he became a counterculture literary icon;[6] he later committed suicide for the reasons people commit suicide: their own overruling of the gift of creation.

But this story and its remarkable voice and precision are still here and still alive.

After I read the story—it's only four printed pages—I quiz my students, asking them which two sentences they believe are the ones I believe are among the most precise descriptions I have ever read; that is, as all good teachers are wont to do, I ask them to read my mind.

The first sentence is this: "My entrance into the thing came about this way: One day I was standing in front of my shack, eating an apple and staring at a black ragged toothache sky."

The second is, "The novelist was in his late forties, tall, reddish, and looked as if life had given him an endless stream of two-timing girlfriends, five-day drunks and cars with bad transmissions."

These are two of the most precise descriptive sentences I have ever encountered, not for the exactitude of their physical or tangible descriptions; in fact, you'll find that the physical element of these descriptions may be merely and only serviceable, indeed might even be a bit vague. But I value these descriptions for their *spiritual* acuity. What happens in these descriptions is that a kind of descriptive triangulation occurs, and by *triangulation* I do not here mean the sort Bill Clinton made famous in his campaigns and subsequent presidency, that surveying of every possible side to be taken and managing somehow to support every one of them. Rather, by *triangulation* I mean the navigation technique that uses the trigonometric properties of triangles to determine a location or course by means of compass bearings from two points a known distance apart.

First, Brautigan gives us descriptive elements that are a known distance apart; that is, we know what a "black" and "ragged" sky looks like (and if you don't, you haven't paid enough attention to the sky). But in giving us that next word, "toothache," he allows us into the unseeable realm of description, the point to which we need to navigate; he gives us the *spirit* of the sky and so the *spirit* of the viewer, a young man eating an apple, the story tells us, who doesn't know what he meant by living the way he did all those years ago. With this word "toothache," we have been placed on a three-dimensional grid and know now not only exactly what the sky looks like but exactly the ache and trouble and mystery of a young man's life.

The same quality of known distances apart holds for the first three descriptors of the novelist: "in his late forties, tall, and reddish." The fact is that these words are, finally, quite dull, and quite vague. If you were a student of mine and used them in a story to describe a character, I would most likely write "ugh" in the margin, which is usually a sign that I think you're not actually trying to write well. But if you were to append this last phrase—"and looked as if life had given him an endless stream of two-timing girlfriends, five-day drunks and cars with bad transmissions"—well, if you wrote that, I'd call you a genius.

Because, as with that toothache sky, we know not only what this guy looks like but also the *spirit* of this man. We could each of us go to a police lineup in which six tall, reddish men in their forties lined up against the wall, and we would know immediately the one with the endless stream of two-timing girlfriends, five-day drunks, and cars with bad transmissions. This is because the description we have been given transcends the physical and leads us into the third dimension in writing: that point when we leave simply *seeing* something and enter into *knowing* that something.

I want to end this pawing through a couple of examples of precise writing as the means by which to learn how to write precisely with an anecdote I haven't written down before but which I am now doing so that I can share with you an extraordinary moment of precision out of my own life. It is a moment that shows me that I serve a precise God in all I do and that teaches me that, because my God is so precise, my writing ought not to be fuzzy or nearly clear or just almost precise enough. My writing ought to be precise because I have been made in the image of God, and not *blurrily* in his image, not *almost* in his image, not *close enough* in his image.

And I tell this story to you—an absolutely true story, nothing I am making up—so that you will know that writing in its largest sense—writing as a matter of living (and I don't mean money), writing as a matter of breathing and seeing, as a matter of *being*—is a matter you will never master, because it is wrought with self-doubt, and steeped in self-doubt, and scoured in self-doubt.

Because writing is a very lonely thing. You do it, and do it, always alone at a desk somewhere, always just spilling words on the page, hoping they will work. Sometimes worldly success enters in—and I have been blessed mightily in this regard—but you are still left with yourself, sitting alone, and trying to write.

This story began on December 13, 2005, a year and a half or so after I had begun my job as editor of *The Southern Review* at Louisiana State University. The last few weeks had been particularly bad for me, not for any personal tragedies but because I was now the editor of this prestigious and influential old journal, and my writing, because of these duties (duties I was glad to take on, as I had hoped to make a dent somehow in the lost world of American letters with editing a quarterly journal), had suffered: I hadn't written in six months. As a consequence, having been away from writing—despite the loneliness of that work—for that long, I had begun to wonder if my writing mattered, if what I was doing even needed doing. What was the point of writing? I began to wonder, and began to wonder if I had made a difference whatsoever.

Then, on December 13, I prayed, in a fit of despair over the whole big thing of being a writer and editor and wondering what the heck I was doing with my life and wondering, as I am sure everyone does, if in fact I were making a difference in anyone's life with my writing and editing. That morning, I prayed to God that, despite how self-centered I was being in asking this, he would give me a sign, that he would somehow let me know that, well, yes, I was making a difference, and that he would do it today. That day, Tuesday, December 13. I know I was being impudent and presumptuous, giving God a deadline. But, I reasoned, I wasn't asking for anything big or for any prizes or recognitions—just word from somewhere that somehow I might be making a difference.

I fully expect answers from God when I pray, as I am a believer in him and in Christ and know from experience that he answers prayers. He doesn't answer them, I also know from much experience, the way I want them to be answered, but answer them he does. Period.

But on that December Tuesday nothing happened—just the same old, same old life I had ground myself into—that of rejecting and rejecting and rejecting manuscripts from well-meaning writers who wanted to be published, and dealing with my staff and their interpersonal problems, and living in a strange city we had never dreamed of living in before I had been offered the job, and all of it cast with the pall of the fact I was not writing. At the end of the day I kept scouring the hours that had just passed in order to see if there were something I had missed, if God's answer to my prayer had been given in some manner I had overlooked, or had come in disguise or so subtly that I had breezed right past it. But there had come no answer to my prayer.

Yet what came to me after I had done all that scouring was a kind of good peace, a peace that—yes—passed all understanding, a peace that let me know that my life was worthy, not because of anything I had written but because Christ died for me, and because God loved me first, and because he had created me. The answer to my prayer, I figured, as I climbed into bed that night, was the deeper understanding that God loved me, and that was enough meaning to last a lifetime.

I got up the next morning, prayed, meditated, read my Bible like I always do, and then, sadly, like I always also do, I went to the computer to check my e-mail.

And here was a letter from someone I didn't know, telling me how a book I had written had deeply affected his life.

I laughed out loud for this answer to my prayer, joyful laughter because of my impudence and presumptuousness to have assumed God would answer me on the day I named, only to have this wonderful e-mail from no one I knew arrive the day after. Here was God first tweaking my nose and then blessing me with exactly what I needed to hear. God works in his own time, I saw, and I laughed.

Then I looked up at the information at the top of the e-mail, that place where all the computer stuff appears, all those numbers and addresses and everything I never really look at.

And guess what?

The man who had written this e-mail, someone I didn't know but to whom my writing had spoken deeply enough to get him to root out my e-mail address, and then sit down to write it and send it, had sent it at 11:59 p.m. on Tuesday, December 13.

At which point my laughter—even though it had sprung from joy at God's humbling me and blessing me at once— disappeared, and I was even more humbled by the fact that God answers even the prayers of the impudent.

But wait: there's more. As if that weren't enough, on Friday, December 16, I received a long letter from a woman who had read another of my books, a letter in which she let me know how deeply that book had spoken to her, how much it meant to her life.

The postmark on the letter? You guessed it: December 13, 2005.

How is that for precision?

And so, as believers, and as those made in God's image, who among us can say, "That's good enough," when we know we haven't given our best to find the exact word for the moment at hand?

To write precisely—and perhaps here is the only how-to you

are going to get out of me—you must *be there*. You must remember you are not writing about this moment, you are not putting words in to substitute for the experience; *you are there*. And while there, you are paying attention; you are at once that cool mathematician taking in the factors available, inserting variables you don't yet know the value of, and working them through to their answer, all while being inside the story you are telling, that is, *all while being the equation itself.*

There. I have finally gotten to writing this essay on precision, and looking back at it now I see it is not the precise thing I wanted it to be. I have only talked around it, tried my best to name it, to put in words the ineffable, and I only hope this has been of some good to you.

But here: one last stab:

Precision calls for patience, it calls for searching; it calls for striving; it also calls for letting yourself trip over what is right there in the path before you. Precision is indispensable; it is just beyond your reach. You don't have the technique, the language, or the courage to achieve precision. But if you want to write, then for all these reasons—and chiefly because we serve a precise God who is creator of all things—you must reach for precision. As a writer you must always be striving for that which you cannot yet achieve and for that which you cannot yet know.

Writing with So Great a Cloud of Witnesses

Last month my best friend, Jeff Deal, and I made a road trip from our hometown of Charleston, South Carolina, to Fort Campbell, Kentucky, to visit my older son, Zebulun, a cavalry scout with the 101st Airborne. Jeff's son Russell is in the army as well, our two boys having made a pact while they were undergrads at Furman University that they would finish college, take a year off, and then join up in order to serve their country in return for the blessing of freedom we have been given and too often take for granted. Both our boys have served their tours of duty in Iraq and come home safely, and now Zeb was getting married in two weeks. I wanted to surprise him, spend some time with him alone, and just be father and son one last time before all in his life changed. And because Jeff, too, is a father who knows what it is to love and miss and pray and worry over a son, he joined me for the eleven-hour drive up to Kentucky and back.

Our families have been friends for over twenty years. Jeff and I have hunted together, fished together, beached his boat out on Drum Island in Charleston Harbor and gone searching for shark's teeth in the beds of dredge pumped out onto the flats of the island. Once, believe it or not, we were stranded in a taxi in a snowstorm in Jordan at the crest of the King's Road, elevation 5,000 feet, on our way from Petra to Aqaba and had to be rescued by the Jordanian army. When my wife, Melanie, and I lived in France, Jeff and his wife, Hart, came and visited us and stayed with us again when we lived in Israel. We went to his mother's funeral in the little Georgia town of Toccoa, where he grew up, one of six children, in a two-room shack. Melanie and I were the only people who weren't family to make the drive from Charleston.

All of which is to say that what Jeff and I talked about on our way home from that quick trip to Fort Campbell wasn't glib, pass-the-time talk. Because we are such close friends, our talk was about what matters to us, and the way we live, and how we parse out and then stitch back together who we are and what we have done and why we do what we do. It was talk borne of a deep and abiding friendship.

And as we drove, the conversation turned to the Heisenberg uncertainty principle. Really.

See, Jeff is the smartest person I know. He recently retired from his practice as one of Charleston's most respected and beloved ear, nose, and throat doctors. But the whole doctor thing, and the smarts it takes to be not only a doctor but also a really good one, is only the tip of the iceberg.

He is a renaissance man. He is a terrific artist—his wildlife drawings have been shown at galleries in Charleston—and he has written and published a novel. He plays the guitar and banjo, both to a fine degree. He is an inventor as well, and one day when you are going in to surgery at a hospital near you, you will be much safer for a device he has created and patented that involves UV light in order to utterly sterilize operating rooms. Though early models of the thing looked like one of those reject droids in the salvage barge in the first *Star Wars* movie, sleeker, cooler models are now in use in a number of hospitals across the country and in Greece and Spain, and a German engineering company is running tests on how it will work as an installation into the lighting systems of hospitals yet to be built. The public hospital system in the United Kingdom is also testing it with an eye toward installing them in fourteen hundred units, and three are already in operation in London.

London, by the way, is where he did a fellowship last year at the London School of Tropical Medicine, this because he wants to better serve people living in South Sudan, where he has spent over a year in toto serving as a doctor in Dinka villages so remote his clinics have at times been kept safe from gun-toting rebels by only a ring of thornbushes.

One more thing (and trust me, this figures in): he is at work on a PhD in anthropology, taking courses at the University of South Carolina with people half his age. He's already written his thesis, though he isn't due to finish coursework for another year, and that thesis—on family structures among the Dinka peoples—is under consideration by Oxford University Press. They asked him to send it to them.

But to Heisenberg: Jeff and I were talking about medical missions and in particular a water missions group with which he is involved and for which Melanie works. Part of the job of installing these water reclamation systems involves surveying how they affect the third-world groups the systems serve; the mission wants to know about life before and after the clean water source has been brought to them—how lives have been changed by that fresh water. Because anthropology is in essence the observation of cultures and societies, we got to talking about the way even an endeavor as benevolent as bringing fresh, drinkable, life-giving water to people who have known only filthy water has the possibility of yielding unwanted and even detrimental results: Who in the village runs the water system, and what power does that convey? What happens to the communal relationships built and maintained by people used to gathering water from riverbanks or traveling together to a distant well, but who now only stand in line in the middle of the village? What of the possible dependence of the people upon the deliverers of the water-purifying machine and the need for those benefactors to maintain the system itself against breakdowns?

And, because Jeff is studying anthropology, he began talking about the observer effect and the way that even surveying people in order to help make certain they are being served as the missions group wishes to serve them is an intrusion, an upsetting of their culture. Simply observing a culture, the observer effect maintains, messes with the culture being observed.

We talked then about the way even thinking about what questions to ask—and what answers perhaps the asker wants to receive—can skew the whole outcome of any such survey. The observer-expectancy effect, or simply observer bias, in which a researcher's perceptions cause him to influence unconsciously the participants of an experiment, can reveal, finally, more about the surveyor than about those being surveyed, not to mention significantly screw up or maybe even destroy the whole experiment. We ask questions we want answers to, and oftentimes we aren't listening to the answers we get because they don't give us what we want to hear, or—even worse—we ask questions that have nothing to do with the real system we are observing.

I know this all sounds abstract, but believe me, we had a fine conversation that applied wholly to the water missions group and its good work, as well as to Jeff's experiences serving the Dinka people and gathering their family stories for his dissertation.

It just so happened that then we started listening to Bill Bryson's book *A Short History of Nearly Everything*, and here came through the speakers words about Heisenberg and his uncertainty principle and the news that, in the effort to predict simultaneously an electron's position and its momentum—the key physical quantities of quantum theory—researchers discovered that when you try to measure one quantity, the other quantity is altered.[1] Trying to measure the velocity of an electron significantly alters its position; measuring its position involves significantly altering its velocity.

Therefore, if one is to try to predict an electron's life, one has to get his head around the fact there is no way to predict an electron's life. Our popular models of electrons as stylized little planets zipping in perfect arcs around an atom are in no way representative of the truth of an electron's path: an electron is nowhere; an electron is everywhere. To try and spot it is to change it.

But while I was sitting behind the wheel of my truck and heading down through the Smokies of eastern Tennessee toward the North Carolina border, there lingered in my ears the notion of surveys of third-world groups, of benevolent endeavors to bring fresh water to people who had none, of the good and bad of monitoring the ways we serve others. Then into this mix came the fact of the impossibility of trying to see and name and measure and touch upon something as elemental as an electron's path, and suddenly I felt click into place an understanding of something that, for a long long long time, has worked on me—I am trying to avoid using the words *bothered me* here—about teaching creative writing. That is, I had an epiphany. The same phenomenon happens in a creative writing workshop as happens in the measuring of an electron's speed, and in the installation of a water system, and in the telling of a Dinka family's story to an anthropologist: there is an intrusion upon the real life of the matter at hand.

I know I am not saying anything new here. Anyone who has had a creative writing workshop knows that external observation and input are part and parcel of the endeavor itself. But what occurred to me, finally, was to ask what effect the workshop has—deeply, truly—on the creation of genuine art.

Don't think I am against workshops. No. I would not be the author of thirteen books if it weren't for a creative writing class I took while I was an RC Cola salesman who'd quit college to pursue a career in soda pop. After a mediocre performance my first two years at Cal State Long Beach, I quit, worked for RC, and saw after a year of *that* that sales wasn't what I wanted to do for the rest of my life. So I enrolled in a course at the local community college because I wanted to get back in the groove of having deadlines and assignments before reenrolling full-time at Cal State that fall. The only night I had free was Tuesday; the only course open on Tuesday nights was creative writing. Here I am.

But I also want to say this: creative writing workshops are about the most unreal model of the writer's life that has ever been concocted. Never in your real life as a writer will a group of people take your writing seriously enough to ask you to write something and then gather together in one place at one time to discuss it with you. Writing is, finally, a matter of being alone and putting words on paper and hoping they will capture as clearly and deeply as humanly possible the sense of what you are seeing and feeling and discovering as you write those words.

Workshops are in and of themselves observer-based phenomena; although they are definitely *not* the generative moment of art, they are predicated on a belief that observation improves output.

I came home from that trip with Jeff and went back to my semester's worth of workshops. But there was something different about the way I looked at my classes, the obtuse angle I suddenly felt between the students and myself, in my head the image of me standing on one side of a canyon, the class on the other, all of them—well, maybe a few of them—furiously writing their hearts out and then waving their stories at me and shouting across the abyss, "What do you think, Mr. Lott?"

I started wondering what they were all thinking about me, the observer of this thing called a creative writing workshop. Then I started to wonder what they thought of the other kids in the class, those other observers who would read their work when it was finished. And then I thought of the fact that some kids in class were friends with each other before they'd ever signed up for the course, while others were absolute strangers to one another. I started wondering about *everything* they were thinking when they wrote these stories.

Of course I had thought of these issues before. Of course I had. But after this particular trip, for the specific purpose of bidding good-bye to my older son, a young man who had been to Iraq and back, who had seen strangers and friends alike killed in the battle-field, and who was now on the eve of entering into the joy and com-fort and upheaval and brand-new world a marriage is, and then to have had this conversation about the ineffable nature of art and time and life with my best friend—well, things were different. *I* was different.

I'd had my epiphany. My role as an instructor was somehow different now.

And just as trying to measure an electron in no way measures an electron, and a dissertation on Dinka family structures in no way captures the Dinka family structure, I'd seen that workshops do not predict, spot, capture, or create art. They cannot. They will not. They won't.

This is because the creation of art is a private affair. It is borne out of solitude, of sitting one's butt flat in a chair at a desk some-where and putting one word after another after another, and seeing through this laborious rote behavior to another world, a dream, a deep vision of an other-life that becomes more alive than the world in which one is sitting and being alone.

Kafka, in his *Letters to Felice,* wrote of this quality of deep pri-vacy, this integral retreat from humanity in order to find the right words that will allow one to make meaningful art that encounters humanity:

> Writing means revealing oneself to excess; that utmost of self-revelation and surrender, in which a human being, when involved with others, would feel he was losing himself, and from which, therefore, he will always shrink as long as he is in his right mind . . . even that degree of self-revelation

and surrender is not enough for writing. Writing that springs from the surface of existence—when there is no other way and the deeper wells have dried up—is nothing, and collapses the moment a truer emotion makes that surface shake. This is why one can never be alone enough when one writes, why there can never be enough silence around when one writes, why even night is not night enough. This is why there is never enough time at one's disposal, for the roads are long and it is easy to go astray.[2]

And as I insert this quotation into this essay, meant as a piece of grand evidence for my argument that workshops alter the generative moment when art arrives, I am thinking that perhaps at the root of all this claptrap about workshops there might very well be a longing for my own writing life of long ago, the one that seemed genuinely to begin only *after* I had graduated way back in 1984 from UMass Amherst with my MFA.

I must admit to my observer bias of the entire creative writing industrial complex from which I draw twice-monthly my very manna, the fact I miss the days when, just after graduating with an MFA buttressed by three years of workshops, I was alone, and had now only to write, and to write.

I miss getting up every morning between 4:30 and 5:00 a.m. and going to the basement of our townhouse apartment in Columbus, Ohio, the city in which I'd gotten a job teaching five sections a quarter of remedial English at Ohio State. Five classes a day, twenty students per class, three quarters a year. Believe it or not, I sorely miss that time way back when I was embarked on writing the first book, what would one day become *The Man Who Owned Vermont*, though my only tangible literary accomplishments at that point were a handful of published stories. I miss that time when I had to sneak down the stairs and avoid a particularly ornery step that would creak so loudly that our then-toddler and only child, Zebulun, would wake up, and the entire endeavor to find quiet would crumble around me.

I miss that aloneness, there at a desk in a basement, where the only window was six feet above the floor, a narrow thing that looked out at ground level and through which I could see stars when I sat down with my mug of instant coffee and piece of toast, before me the life of an RC Cola salesman and the landscape of western Massachusetts, his sales route, and the shambles of his marriage.

Though I get up at 5:30 every day still and go to my desk to write—I am in the middle of my fifteenth book—I miss that time, because then, no one—no one—was watching me write. I was the only one on planet earth who cared about what was going to happen to this RC salesman; no one else even knew about this guy, and each morning down in that basement were words about him waiting just beyond my reach, words that, if I just listened closely enough to this salesman, would allow me to grab hold of them and put them in the order his actions and thoughts and *heart* showed me was the right way.

Maybe that's where all this comes from: my longing for that time before I'd ever written a single book, that time when it seemed, for a while, night was night enough.

So, what did I do with my epiphany about teaching creative writing?

Despite my so-recent realization of the risks of observation, I decided to observe what I was observing: I wrote a questionnaire and took a survey of my students, not only of my own students but also of creative writing students in other classes at the College of Charleston. Carol Ann Davis passed it out to her poetry workshop, and Tony Varallo passed it out to his fiction workshop, and I gave it to my creative nonfiction workshop and to my advanced fiction workshop.

I am not in the habit of taking surveys. I don't like them, because it seems their aim is to find the average, the mean, the lowest common denominator among that being measured, while as a writer of fiction I'm trying to traffic in the anomaly, the out-of-the-norm, even when I'm writing about what generally interests me: normal people (such as they are). And though my bias against surveys runs so deep that when I was hired by the college in 1986, I refused to take the mandatory Myers-Briggs personality assessment chiefly because I don't want to know what type I am, my bias still didn't stop me from conducting *my* survey, because *I* was the one who wanted to get to the heart of my students and to know what they were thinking of when they were in the private moment of generating a story, an essay, or a poem. What *I* wanted to know was important stuff.

My questionnaire was a beautifully crafted thing: twelve questions (1. "When I am writing a story, essay, or poem for a workshop, I think about the response the work might receive from the workshop as a whole," etc.) that sought on a scale of 1 ("Never") to 5 ("I think a great deal about it, and let it influence my work to a large degree") to pierce the mysterious penumbra of the privacy of writing. There was also an introduction simultaneously funny, disarming, smart, and heartfelt (". . . I want honest answers to these questions, and no beret-wearing, clove cigarette–smoking, cappuccino-sipping *I'm an artist!* heroics: the art of writing insists upon an inner honesty that is coldly ruthless in its assessment of why we do what we do, both in life and in the creation of art. No posing allowed. Tell the truth."). I even had a section of questions for people who'd been in workshops before the one they were in right now.

It was a beautiful thing. And preposterously stupid and sadly self-serving.

I received fifty responses, had to throw out two (one because the respondent wrote "zero" in a couple of places instead of using the point scale; the other because the respondent didn't bother to read the questionnaire and simply wrote yes or no), and found from the forty-eight students left that, well, yes, above all, when they are writing a story, a poem, or an essay, they are thinking of the teacher's response (3.7 on my 1 to 5 scale). Next in line was the fact they are thinking of the workshop response as a whole (3.0), and coming in third was their thinking of the response the piece would elicit from a specific prior workshop instructor (2.5).

No news here. Students are thinking, in the moment of trying to create art, of the instructor, both present and past, and about those around them in the classroom. Of course, the response I would get would be the response I was looking for, though I'd hoped for something different: that our students would be writing only toward the story or poem or essay they were in the midst of creating, trying to let it be itself instead of fashioned with an eye toward the others there in the classroom with them.

But.

A day after the class meeting in which I'd administered the survey, I got an e-mail from a student in one of my workshops. One Lauren Capone, a graduating senior from New Orleans who was planning to take off a year before applying—if she decided she really wanted and needed it—to an MFA program.

It was a long e-mail, one I very much enjoyed for its candor, its clear-eyed freshness of thought. "I found my way into writing late in high school," she wrote. "I wasn't quite sure what I was doing with it; it was the summer after senior year, and I recall simply wanting to get out of the house so I went to coffee shops all day and wrote, or made small sketches in a notebook. I didn't share it with anyone and not because it was private, just because it didn't come to me to do so." She also told of how she sort of backed into workshops: "For a while I took drawing classes, photography, then printmaking. But what I found was that the writing was always there. And that of all mediums, it had the potential to contain me, whereas with something like photography, I felt it was too easy and that I could control most everything. So I started considering writing classes."

And because my mission in giving this survey was to try and figure in my sadly academic, 1-to-5-point way what my students were thinking when writing, I quote the following assessment of the worth of a writing workshop, with her permission:

> The difficulty with workshops is that the written thing is so big, and often treated as a completed piece of writing, when in fact, at least in my case, I am well aware that it needs more work. Additionally I've become less and less concerned with the finished product itself and more in it for the practice of writing, and the discoveries therein. I can sometimes benefit from a workshop if it addresses possibilities for further development of the piece; things to try with the writing. As for people feeling confused [about a story], I for one do not frequently think about the fact that someone might be reading the piece. So in class when peers are confused by something, these kinds of things can be helpful [to the author], but judgment calls are difficult. I don't think that we ought to be given these kinds of things that we can grasp onto like a flotation device, I think [a story] needs to be self-perpetuated, because in the world, you don't get these pillows to rest on, you must find them yourself and keep plugging along. With some mental work I've become pretty good with quieting the distracting judgments that can arise in my mind while I am trying to write.

No number my wonderful survey yielded struck me as more on the mark as to the role the workshop ought to have in the creation of art than this remarkable offering made by a student I was doing my best to observe as part of a classroom of students; her e-mail quashed beautifully any further notion I had of asking a pile of stupid questions about what they were thinking about workshops.

So what ought a workshop to be?

When I was a graduate student at UMass, I had the great good fortune to be selected to participate in a creative writing workshop taught by James Baldwin. The class was made up of three students from each of the Five Colleges (UMass Amherst, Amherst College, Smith College, Mount Holyoke, and Hampshire College), and we eager students became aware pretty quickly that Mr. Baldwin wasn't much of a workshop instructor. He'd never been in one, much less taught one, and when after turning in our stories and showing up the next week expecting exquisite assessments of the work at hand and how we might make it better, we were sorely disappointed. He had no vocabulary for this endeavor; he had no spirit for it; he had no means by which to impart to us, from the wellspring of the creation of his own art, the sorts of things we wanted to hear from him: how to improve the dialogue, the setting, the structure, the characters, the plot.

All that technical stuff *we* wanted to talk about.

The problem, we classmates soon realized (among us, though in our chrysalis stages, the novelist Susan Straight and the playwright Suzan-Lori Parks) was with ourselves. We were seeking from him what he could not give; we were expectant electrons in a system waiting to be observed. But he wasn't even looking at us.

This was because he was a *writer* and not a trafficker in matters of technique.

After a few weeks of this charade called a workshop *we* were putting *him* through, Mr. Baldwin, a soul at once as meek and as dignified as I have ever encountered, turned out to have been giving us something we hadn't been looking for at all, a system we weren't a part of because it was a system we hadn't been interested in. He began to talk to us about art and literature and their importance, relevance, and necessity within the life of the writer. He spoke of the need to write, the need to keep writing no matter what, and the redemptive quality a life in art might afford us.

And though we ended up without a clue as to how to make our stories better, we received an extraordinary education nonetheless.

Now *that* was a good workshop.

In 1981 I read *What We Talk About When We Talk About Love*, my first encounter with the work of Raymond Carver and the way he rendered with awesome precision the razor-edge lives of people who might fall apart at any moment or who might very well hang on to the bitter end.[3] I saw people who mattered to me and saw that the author's job was to get out of the way of these people and let them speak for themselves, for better and worse, on their way through their own stories.

That was a good workshop, too.

And even the traditional workshop, the sort I've been taking to task with all these words, can be a good workshop. One autumn Tuesday afternoon in Amherst, I walked into the second class meeting of Jay Neugeboren's workshop. Neugeboren is a writer whose stories and books were legend among us. I'd handed in my story the week before and sat down to see my work examined in the most traditional of ways, each student there weighing in one way and another, Jay patiently leading and prodding, then stepping up at the end with his own two cents.

He liked it. He suggested this and that, things here and there. He suggested ways to make it a better story in the traditional ways a workshop teacher can suggest. More importantly, the careful and generous and even-handed way in which he let us express our views and then expressed his own made me a better writer, one who could sit alone and write stories those early mornings and then feel confident that the response they might receive in class would be just, and genuine, and true. His workshop was a gift to me and led to my choosing him to be the mentor of my work while at UMass.

The story I turned in? A little thing—seven pages—about a rocky moment within a young marriage. "I Owned Vermont" would be its eventual title.

Hebrews 12:1 is a verse that comes at the end of a passage in which Paul exhorts his readers to remember everyone of faith— from Abel to Abraham to Moses to Rahab to the nameless men and women martyred through the ages—and their perseverance in that faith: "Therefore, since we are surrounded by so great a cloud of witnesses, let us lay aside every weight, and sin which clings so closely, and let us run with endurance the race that is set before us."

The witnesses—that great cloud—aren't, as is often thought, some sort of swirling mass of spirit entities watching what we are doing as we do it, so that you better watch out, you better not cry, you better not pout, Paul's telling you why. No. Rather, what is meant by the word "witness" here is the quality of the lives lived before ours; the measure of faith and life in that faith that each brought to his or her relationship to our creator God; it is the example, if I may, of the artistry by which each lived his or her life in service to that God.

I think, finally, that the best workshop we can have might very well be with our own cloud of witnesses, people who went before us *and* people who are still among us, whose lives in art—whose giving of fresh and enlivening water through their words—most affect us.

My witnesses include Baldwin and Carver and Neugeboren. But chief among them has to be Flannery O'Connor, who wrote:

> One thing that is always with the writer—no matter how long he has written or how good he is—is the continuing process of learning how to write. As soon as the writer "learns to write," as soon as he knows what he is going to find, and discovers a way to say what he knew all along, or worse still, a way to say nothing, he is finished. If a writer is any good, what he makes will have its source in a realm much larger than that which his conscious mind can encompass and will always be a greater surprise to him that it can ever be to his reader.[4]

Yet another key witness for me is John Steinbeck, who wrote on the eighteenth day of the journal he kept while writing *The Grapes of Wrath*—he completed the book in one hundred days—"If only I could do this book properly it would be one of the really fine books and a truly American book. But I am assailed with my own ignorance and inability. I'll just have to work from a background of these."[5] I come in close contact with my own ignorance and inability every time I touch the keyboard, and to know Steinbeck wrote that book in full embrace of his own gives me the courage I need to move forward, in spite of me.

Perhaps the newest member of this workshop of witnesses is Lauren Capone, who reminds me that it takes mental work to quiet the distracting judgments that arise when I am trying to write.

This is because writing occurs within an immeasurable moment, in the privacy of the way synapses fire within the brain, layering one snap onto another until an image occurs, begins to breathe, then stands up and walks its way through nerves into muscles into the fingertips and onto the hard plastic of a keyboard, or through the smallest kiss of a pen on paper.

This moment is incredibly brittle, ready to break at the smallest creak of a stairway step or gulp of cold coffee. To call this act of synapse to fingertips "writing" is to describe it in the most rudimentary way, revealing to no real extent what the engaged imagination is in the act of doing: creating a new world.

What I think I may be understanding, now that the whole of this moment of measuring the immeasurable is over, now that my clever numbers have been recorded and tossed away, is that the business I ought to be about in the workshops I teach is to be not only the teacher but also a writer, there at my desk at 5:30 each morning with my coffee and the next new world I am imagining. As the observer observing, I must first and foremost be the best witness I can be.

As I write this, Zeb is now married. Jeff Deal is in Honduras, working to provide potable water to villagers high in the mountains. A new flare-up of tribal killings has occurred in Wernyol in South Sudan, and the weather this moment on the King's Road to Aqaba is a warm 88 degrees.

That is, the electron-world is busy spinning, being itself.

And I am here, however preposterously stupid or sadly self-serving, writing this; trying to find with each word when night is night enough; trying to write, and to be writing.

Humble Flannery

Flannery O'Connor is, of course, the de facto patron saint of creative writing. It's pretty difficult to get through an education in writing, whether self-inflicted or programmed into you via a university education, without meeting someone—and maybe *being* someone—who strikes a match and lights a votive candle at the mention of her name.

But sometimes the kind of reverence a lot of people hold for her and her work is tough to reconcile with the ornery, even acerbic tone one finds in her writing, especially in many of the essays that make up *Mystery and Manners*. For instance, there's this tough little indictment from O'Connor of everyone in every creative writing program in the world: "Everywhere I go I'm asked if I think the universities stifle writers," she wrote in "The Nature and Aim of Fiction." "My opinion is they don't stifle enough of them. There's many a best-seller that could have been prevented by a good teacher. The idea of being a writer attracts a good many shiftless people, those who are merely burdened by poetic feelings or afflicted with sensibility."[1]

And if anyone out there is wondering why talk about Flannery O'Connor still continues, why she is someone, though dead these last forty-eight years, whose words are worthy enough of our attention to this day, here's a little factoid to chew on: she was only the second twentieth-century writer to have her work collected for the Library of America series. This means her work was more quickly recognized for its enduring influence and importance than the works of subsequently published Library of America volumes by such writers as F. Scott Fitzgerald, John Steinbeck, Eugene O'Neill, John Dos Passos, Zora Neale Hurston, Eudora Welty, and even Robert Frost—all writers whose careers were well under way (and for some even over) before O'Connor ever published a story. Hemingway, by the way, appears in only an assortment of anthologies put out by the LOA. The first twentieth-century writer, the only one in *front* of Miss O'Connor? None other than William Faulkner.

Yet the fact remains that what Flannery had to say about writing can at times seem at least troublesome, at most downright cruel. Or, as David Madden wrote in an essay about O'Connor's influence on his life, "Sometimes, as a person and as a person who is a writer, I think I need O'Connor like I need a hole in the head; but sometimes I think that is exactly what I need, and O'Connor is only too happy to oblige me."[2]

Yet what has come to me, the slow learning votive bearer that I am, through all these years of reading and rereading and re-rereading her work is that her seemingly belligerent observations about the writing life aren't rooted in any sort of arrogance or disdain regarding those who wish to practice the art; rather, her words point to a kind of hard-wrought humility she was after, letting those who want to write know they need. Here are the opening paragraphs of "The Nature and Aim of Fiction":

> I understand that this is a course called "How the Writer Writes," and that each week you are exposed to a different writer who holds forth on the subject. The only parallel I can think of to this is having the zoo come to you, one animal at a time; and I suspect that what you hear one week from the giraffe is contradicted the next week by the baboon.
>
> My own problem in thinking what I should say to you tonight has been how to interpret such a title as "How the Writer Writes." In the first place, there is no such thing as

THE WRITER, and I think that if you don't know that now, you should by the time such a course as this is over. In fact, I predict that it is the one thing you can be absolutely certain of learning.[3]

In these words we see blatantly the core of Flannery O'Connor's life in relation to words, both nonfiction (and I include here her letters) and fiction. With the words "there is no such thing as THE WRITER," she heralds the battle that all writers of any merit fight daily, indeed the battle they fight with each next word they put to paper.

The battle is this: the *dethroning* of the writer, the constant and all-consuming bloody coup every story or poem or essay—every genuine work of art—must accomplish over its author in order truly to live and to breathe and to have something to say to us that will matter. It was a battle O'Connor fought her entire writing life, a battle for the story's preeminence over its writer—an incredibly humble stance to take but a necessary one, she knew, because she knew we are all of us, finally, not our own creation, but created beings whose lives are lived in constant tension between the Creator and the created, whether we believe in God or not. In "Novelist and Believer," she writes:

> At its best our age is an age of searchers, and at its worst, an age that has domesticated despair and learned to live with it happily. The fiction which celebrates this last state will be the least likely to transcend its limitations, for when the religious need is banished successfully, it usually atrophies, even in the novelist. The sense of mystery vanishes. A kind of reverse evolution takes place, and the whole range of feeling is dulled.[4]

It is this mystery she refers to that is the humbling circumstance, the humbling *presence* that keeps the true writer humble; and for Flannery, this mystery is an extension of God that signals one is attuned to true creation, and hence to the Creator.

Letters

But the problem with Flannery O'Connor is that this battle *for* humility oftentimes comes off sounding to our ears as pompous, as arrogant, sometimes even rude. Not to mention terribly funny.

And there's plenty of funny in her words about writing and its study. Here's a passage from a letter she wrote in May of 1959 to Dr. Ted R. Spivey, a professor at Georgia State University who became a lifelong correspondent with O'Connor after having visited her in Milledgeville the year before. She writes to him:

> Week before last I went to Wesleyan and read "A Good Man Is Hard to Find." After it I went to one of the classes where I was asked questions. There were a couple of young teachers there, and one of them, an earnest type, started asking the questions. "Miss O'Connor," he said, "why is the Misfit's hat *black?*" I said most countrymen in Georgia wore black hats. Then he said, "Miss O'Connor, the misfit represents Christ, does he not?" "He does not," I said. He looked crushed. "Well, Miss O'Connor," he said, "what is the significance of the Misfit's hat?" I said it was to cover his head, and after that he left me alone.[5]

And there is this opening paragraph from "On Her Own Work," remarks given in 1962 at Hollins College as an introduction to a reading of "A Good Man Is Hard to Find":

> Last fall I received a letter from a student who said she would be "graciously appreciative" if I would tell her "just what enlightenment" I expected her to get from each of my stories. I suspect she had a paper to write. I wrote her back to forget about the enlightenment and just try to enjoy them. I knew that was the most unsatisfactory answer I could have given because, of course, she didn't want to enjoy them, she just wanted to figure them out.
>
> In most English classes the short story has become a kind of literary specimen to be dissected. Every time a story of mine appears in a Freshman anthology, I have a vision of it, with its little organs laid open, like a frog in a bottle.[6]

Once, when asked by a student why she wrote, she responded, "Because I'm good at it."

On the surface, her responses to these inquiries into her own intentions, however humorous, might seem laced with scornful condescension, exhibiting nothing like a humble stance. But upon a little closer examination of the questions and her responses, one can see that what O'Connor is saying, in her own gruff way, is "Forget about me! Read the story! That's where you'll find everything you'll need to understand it!" It is to the work she has made that she wants eyes to turn and not to the personality behind it.

In this way her humility is a fierce, almost combative one, because she knows how deeply important this humility is, and knows that it is the work one creates that is paramount. "A story is a way to say something that can't be said any other way," she writes in "Writing Short Stories," "and it takes every word in the story to say what the meaning is. You tell a story because a statement would be inadequate. When anybody asks what a story is about, the only proper thing to tell him is to read the story. The meaning of fiction is not abstract meaning but experienced meaning."[7]

Her humility had to be just as loud, just as "grotesque," as it were, as those larger-than-life characters she created in her stories. As she put it in "The Fiction Writer and His Country," "When you can assume that your audience holds the same beliefs that you do, you can relax a little and use more normal means of talking to it; when you have to assume it does not, then you have to make your vision apparent by shock—to the hard of hearing you shout, and for the almost blind you draw large and startling figures."[8] O'Connor knew she had to divert those interested in *her* because of the perception that the writer is the god of theme and symbol and meaning of the story itself. Even her humility, it follows, had to be shouted, had to be writ large for the nearly blind in order best to speak to a time in which not only religious need had begun to atrophy, but even humility itself.

Letters

And as I wrote the sentence I have just written, I couldn't help but think of this day and age, right here and now, in which being famous for being famous is the flag of the day, and here come the escapades of the Kardashians, the guido culture of *Jersey Shore*, and the lives ahead for Jon and Kate's eight. We are as a culture more blind than ever we were when Flannery wrote about the mystery vanishing; reverse evolution is now fully in place, and all one need do to be a beacon of culture is to be pee between cars in a parking lot while the paparazzi snap away.

Which is why I find O'Connor's candor so refreshing, her hellfire and brimstone brand of humility so bracing. Because she knew that a story—any work of art—is a manifestation of the eternal and far more important than the artist can ever be. A work of art is a foray into the Holy of Holies; it is an approaching of the mystery she held so dear.

Of this mystery inherent to any true work of art, Tolstoy wrote, "The most important thing in a work of art is that it should have a kind of focus—i.e., some place where all the rays meet or from which they issue. And this focus must not be capable of being completely explained in words."[9] Any talk about that mystery, therefore, so as to disassemble a story in order to "figure it out" is moot, and perhaps even more than that, to Flannery's way of thinking: it is a violation of the story's sovereignty, the academic equivalent of ransacking the temple of its gold, then melting it down and casting it into that special kind of golden calf we call a term paper, critical thesis, or dissertation.

She believed in the art over the artist, for she knew intimately that the artist was a human, rife with his own failures and prejudices, and his days fleeting at best. She understood that the story would be what remained—not on the shelf of a library somewhere, and not as a citation in a book of critical theory, but as a residual element of the soul of the story's maker. And so the story, in service to its truest Creator, had better be good, and had better speak loud and clear about what matters.

And because art is a manifestation of the eternal, and because so very much is at stake in the creating of art, Flannery O'Connor knew the eternal had to be approached on one's knees; it had to be approached humbly, carefully, cautiously. But I also believe she knew the eternal had to be approached boldly and without fear, just as paradoxically the Christian must, in Paul's words, both "work out [his] own salvation with fear and trembling" (Phil. 2:12) and at the same time "draw near to the throne of grace, that we may receive mercy" (Heb. 4:16).

Once again I return to "The Nature and Aim of Fiction," an essay no student of mine ever gets through my classes without reading, and the moment when humble Flannery puts the finest point possible on the necessity of humility to the creation of true art:

> One of the most common and saddest spectacles is that of a person of really fine sensibility and acute psychological perception trying to write fiction by using these qualities alone. This type of writer will put down one intensely emotional or keenly perceptive sentence after the other, and the result will be complete dullness. The fact is that the materials of the fiction writer are the humblest. Fiction is about everything human and we are made out of dust, and if you scorn getting yourself dusty, then you shouldn't try to write fiction. It's not a grand enough job for you.[10]

The humble recognition that we are all made of dust is the primary element of humility; we can't approach mystery at an esoteric and abstract remove from the smelly rabble of which we are all of us a part. And if there is any approach to be made to the eternal, to the mystery, to that which in a work of art "must not be able to be completely explained in words," it has to come through a confrontation with that rabble; it has to come through a confrontation with the concrete reality of humankind. It has to come through a confrontation with ourselves.

This concrete reality is the depravity of man; she is speaking here of facing the cold hard fact of our being fallen creatures and not simply misunderstood victims, as so much of our literature these days propounds we are. In a letter, O'Connor wrote, "Fiction is supposed to represent life, and the fiction writer has to use as many aspects of life as are necessary to make his total picture convincing. The fiction writer doesn't state, he shows, renders. It's the nature of fiction and it can't be helped. If you're writing about the vulgar, you have to prove they're vulgar by showing them at it."[11]

Even the most cursory look at O'Connor's own fiction will reveal to the reader her willingness to get dusty; that is, to render acutely and coldly and vividly the most seemingly black-hearted—the most vulgar—of characters. In this regard she operated fearlessly, gleefully even; think not only of The Misfit, but also of those quintessential good ole boys Hiram and Bobby Lee grinning and joshing as they walk the family back into the woods; think of pretty much anyone you want in *Wise Blood;* think of the Bible salesman with his deck of nasty cards and that hijacked leg in "Good Country People," and morose college grad Julian in "Everything That Rises Must Converge," a wannabe writer who lives with his proud and doting mother and who spends most of his time in the "inner compartment of his mind," a place his mother has never entered but from which he believes he can view her with "absolute clarity."

And think of Mr. Head in "The Artificial Nigger" and his betrayal of his young grandson Nelson with perhaps the coldest words she ever penned: "This is not my boy," Mr. Head says to the threatening crowd of Atlanta housewives gathered around him, his grandson holding tight to his leg in the hopes his grandfather will protect him from these harridans at the deepest circle of hell. "I never seen him before," Mr. Head says, and walks away from the boy, the women "staring at him with horror, as if they were so repulsed by a man who could deny his own image and likeness that they could not bear to lay hands on him."[12]

But here yet again is a paradox: it is only *through* the confronta-

tion with depravity—that humble dust of which we are all made—
that the moment of mystery will be allowed to arrive. O'Connor writes
in "On Her Own Work," "I have found that violence is strangely capable of returning my characters to reality and preparing them to
accept their moment of grace. Their heads are so hard that almost
nothing else will do the work."[13] It is only once that confrontation
with the concrete reality of man has ruined us that we are allowed to
pierce that reality so that we might receive our impending moment
of grace, a moment in which we reach that ineffable place where all
the rays meet or from which they issue, before being thrown back
into our depraved reality to see what happens next.

It's quite a moment when finally, through dint of violence that
reveals self to self, light in all its cold and scouring glory streams
into the eyes of one or another of O'Connor's hard-headed gro-
tesques. Here is the closing of "Everything That Rises Must Converge," when that arrogant Julian—the college grad who wants to
be a *writer*—sees his mother stagger away from an assault on her
out on the sidewalk of a neighborhood nowhere near home, Julian
complicit in her impending death because of his inability to see the
assault as anything but what she deserved, until now, when he real-
izes the depth of his betrayal:

> Stunned, he let her go and she lurched forward again, walk-
> ing as if one leg were shorter than the other. A tide of dark-
> ness seemed to be sweeping her from him. "Mother!" he
> cried. "Darling, sweetheart, wait!" Crumpling, she fell to the
> pavement. He dashed forward and fell at her side, crying,
> "Mamma! Mamma!" He turned her over. Her face was fiercely
> distorted. One eye, large and staring, moved slightly to the
> left as if it had become unmoored. The other remained fixed
> on him, raked his face again, found nothing and closed.
>
> "Wait here, wait here!" he cried and jumped up and began
> to run for help toward a cluster of lights he saw in the dis-
> tance ahead of him. "Help! Help!" he shouted, but his voice
> was thin, scarcely a thread of sound. The lights drifted far-

ther away the faster he ran and his feet moved numbly as if
they carried him nowhere. The tide of darkness seemed to
sweep him back to her, postponing from moment to moment
his entry into the world of guilt and sorrow.[14]

Only through the violence of his mother's death is Julian allowed
to begin to be a human, geared up finally with a broken heart and
dirty hands.

I'd like to turn now, as a means to begin the march home to the
end of this Flannery fete, to the question of what role O'Connor's
being a southern writer might have to do with all this religion-like
humility, a question that steers perilously close to the old one about
what makes a southern writer southern. It's a silly question, finally,
and pretty much worn out. I once heard Barry Hannah say, "There's
no such thing as a southern writer. There's only a person who writes
one good sentence, then another one, then another one." I couldn't
agree more.

But in 1968 the *Southern Review* published the first of its special issues called Writing in the South (there have been seventeen
thus far) as a means not to try and explain southern writing but to
allow its readers to witness its many voices and forms. And for that
first issue Walter Sullivan, novelist, essayist, and a beloved professor of literature at Vanderbilt, wrote an essay called "In Time of the
Breaking of Nations: The Decline of Southern Fiction." The piece
is a remarkably frank appraisal of the current state of affairs in
southern fiction, albeit forty-five years ago. But it is striking in its
assertion as to who, really, was the only genuine article in the prior
twenty years of southern literature. Yet what is most remarkable, I
believe, is *why* he believes this to be the case. He writes:

Some of the attributes of the traditional South remain and
many of them are rich in drama. They can be used by the
novelist: but they will have to be used. All the crazy characters in the South; all the sense of the past; all the manners

good and bad; all the woods and fields and streams are only empty vessels now and they will have to be filled and re-formed according to each individual writer's own metaphysic. And the Southern writer had better stop allowing himself to be misled. For the past twenty years [1948–1968], young authors coming to maturity have congratulated themselves on being born in Tennessee or Alabama or Mississippi or Georgia, lands that they can both hate and love, countries of rich tradition and tall tales. But the self-praise was premature: living under the shadow of the giants of the renaissance and trying to follow in their footsteps, the young writers have largely failed. The significant exception is Flannery O'Connor whose voice was the only distinctly new and original one yet to arise in the post renaissance South. Recently, a Midwestern writer, and a very good one, visited Nashville, which was his first trip to the South since his early college days. He saw how much and how little the South had changed since his last visit, how much and how little it resembled the country depicted in the renaissance novels and stories he had read. Finally, he announced that he was now certain of what on his arrival he had held only as a tentative judgment: that Flannery O'Connor was a Catholic writer, not a Southern writer at all.

There is much truth in this conclusion; however Southern she was, she was first a Catholic and that made all the difference. And if the Southern renaissance is to have a new flowering, this is what the new generation of writers must understand. The South, important as it still may be as a ground of action, is no longer the prime mover, the first principle on which a literary career may be built. Like Flannery O'Connor, the new Southern writer must be something other than Southern: his faith and his vision must be fixed somewhere beyond the Southern experience: he must find his own source. Only then can he bring the old images alive once more.[15]

This is quite an assertion, his belief that the southern writer had better be something other than southern, and it is one with which I agree. But in this text, Flannery O'Connor serves to exemplify the true artist's ability to transcend his or her own South and, through that transcendence, to return to that South in order best to illuminate, not southernness but the human condition—fallen man—in relation not only to those southern streams and fields and crazy characters but also, and of course most importantly, to his Creator.

But I also believe that this same necessary transcendence of the self in order to find the self will hold true for every writer—not just the southern one—who is willing to see humbly enough that putting one word after another and another won't make one a writer (there is no such thing as THE WRITER, remember), but that it will leave its residual element in the soul; it will leave its mystery.

The battle to get out of the way of oneself is a worthy one, and bloody, and usually results in sore knees and dirty hands. But it can also result in that mystery and in touching upon it, and what better moment might there be than that?

Miller Williams, in an essay called simply enough, "Remembering Flannery O'Connor," tells of when he was a young textbook salesman for Harcourt Brace living and working out of Macon, Georgia, and how he simply decided one day to visit her at Andalusia on the strength of his being a rep for the house that published her work.

The portrait of her is a moving one, and shows her to be tender, and generous, and patient with this young writer. It is complete with lemonade shared with her on the screened porch at Andalusia, and with her giving gentle advice regarding the fledgling poet's work; there are even quiet moments while the two of them watch Williams's daughter chase the peacocks around the front lawn. It's a portrait of Miss O'Connor we don't often get, even in her letters.

While he visited her, he was careful to make note of her words to him regarding writing: her suggestions, her instruction, her wisdom.

"Tell the truth, but understand that it is not necessarily what happened," is one of the things she told him. "Every good story is a parable," is another.

And there is this: "Don't let anyone or anything cut into your time with words."[16]

That's the one I wrote down myself, after having read Williams's essay, the wisdom passed from her to me via words on a page, wisdom against which one cannot argue.

Don't let anyone or anything cut into your time with words.

I wrote it on a yellow Post-it note, and it is taped to the wall above my desk. The ink has faded near to nothing for the number of years I have had it up there. And of course my God and my relationship to him—as with Flannery—will always come first; there is then my wife and children and our walk in Christ.

But each morning when I pray before I begin my work with words, I pray this prayer, square in the face of the ravening world around me that would keep me from that mystery available through my time with words, a prayer I pray daily in the face of a world that will dupe me into believing in me every chance it will ever get.

Part 2

LIFE

At Some Point in the Future, What Has Not Happened Will Be in the Past

1

will have had

Three words I write in the margin of a student's story. He's an exchange student from Germany, a kid who wears death metal T-shirts to my creative writing class. His name is Achim Partheymueller.

I cannot make this up.

He's written a story about the end of the world. A funny story, a crazy story, a moving story: the television reports an asteroid is headed for earth and will hit in 112 minutes, and the jaded young people who inhabit this story set out to see what's happening outside their apartment. In the streets people are partying, rioting, looting, and crying, and the narrator and his friends make their way through the mayhem to a park, where there's a swing set. At this point the narrator remembers playing on swings just like these when he was a child, and the last sentence of the story cuts off without ending, right in the middle of the narrator's memory of being a child on a swing. The end has come.

It's around 9:30 in the evening, and I am in my leather chair in the sitting room of my home here in Hanahan, South Carolina, marking up stories for tomorrow's class, in this instant correcting a verb tense—the future perfect—a couple paragraphs in. It's a form

Life

Achim hasn't found or isn't confident enough to use, I imagine, because English is his second language.

will have had, I scribble.

Then I am hit with it, square in the heart, and I begin, for lack of any better, more elegant, more poetic or sensible or proprietary word I know, to describe what is happening, to cry.

This is another essay about the death of a father.

2

I wrote the above words eleven months ago. April 2008. I haven't come back to them since.

My father died July 9, 2006, so even those few sentences took nearly two years to get to.

Today is March 2, 2009.

Wilman Sequoia Lott.

My literary hero, Raymond Carver, once wrote, "If the writing can't be made as good as it is within us to make it, then why do it? In the end, the satisfaction of having done our best, and the proof of that labor, is the one thing we can take into the grave."

Thank you, Raymond Carver, for making me see I must do my best with the writing of this.

And thank you, Achim Partheymueller, for having gotten me to begin writing this down.

3

I am in downtown Denver and walking back to my hotel after having been the keynote speaker at an annual book awards ceremony. It's a little after 10:00 this Saturday night—July 8, 2006—and a light mist is falling, the thin air out here cooler than I'd thought it would be. My hotel is only a block or so from the venue, and I am alone, and I am talking to myself.

"This is another essay about the death of a father," I say in rhythm with my steps. I say it again and again and again, my eyes

96

to the sidewalk, to the night skyline, to the darkened windows of the buildings I pass.

He hasn't died yet. Not yet. But it's coming, I know. It's coming. One day I will begin writing down this story, and this will be a sentence I will use.

Yesterday I flew here from Baton Rouge, where I work as the editor of a literary journal, and have spent this entire day inside my room at the hotel. Room service, breakfast and lunch. I sat on the king bed and wrote the whole speech—almost fifteen pages—on my laptop, then printed it out in the business center on the first floor, then went to the dinner and delivered those words.

I may have made some friends with what I said to the celebrants, but I am afraid I may have made more enemies than anything else. The awards are for the best Christian novels published in the prior year, and I fear I was the new son-in-law at his first family reunion who systematically insults every family member he meets. Though I am a Christian, I have never been to one of these gatherings before, because I don't write what most Christians would call "Christian fiction." I felt myself the odd man out the whole evening long.

"I am calling for an attitude of reverence and awe for the written word by all parties involved," I have said in a dining room suitably elegant and festive and jammed with happy authors and publishers and booksellers who are Christians and who all seem to know one another.

"I fear we live in a day when we are feeding on Christian fiction as a child feeds on milk," I said to them all.

And I said to the gathered, "Unless we create fiction that does more than simply entertain the troops—unless we make room within the Christian writing industrial complex for writers to create worthy work—art—that in its craftsmanship and vision challenges the heart and soul and mind of our readers—then we will be nothing more than happy clowns juggling for one another."

People came to me and thanked me once it was over. Many

more people stayed away. What I told them all is something I was moved deeply to say, and now that I have said it, I am afraid none of it matters. I am afraid that people will do what they want and to their own ends. I am afraid that the real purpose of writing books, whether Christian or not, is to sell books, and that the way to sell books is to write books that give people what they already know. I fear that the best way to sell a book is to write one that meets a reader's expectations of what a book ought to be rather than to write something that might challenge and surprise and unseat the reader from his throne seat of Me.

Now I am talking to myself, because I am very much alone on the face of this earth, and because my father is back in the hospital tonight, and because I am afraid he is dying.

He is a diabetic and has been for the last thirty years. He has taken insulin shots for just as long. He has had a toe removed. He is losing his vision. He has had problems with blood circulation in his legs and sores that will not heal in his feet, and he has been hospitalized several times in the last two years.

Last night in my hotel room I got a call from my wife, Melanie, at home in Louisiana telling me he had been brought back to the hospital from the rehabilitation center we'd checked him into just four days before. He'd been taken to the hospital for a scheduled round of dialysis, but when the doctor saw his left leg and the sore there gone hugely bad, he'd decided to amputate it.

My parents live in Sequim, Washington, out on the Olympic Peninsula, having retired there in 2003 after fifty years in Southern California. My dad, in those Los Angeles days of yore and plenty, was first a furniture mover; then a truck driver for Nehi; an RC Cola salesman; then RC supervisor; then RC vice president; then chain salesman for Coca-Cola; a supervisor for Dr. Pepper; and, finally, a food broker for in-house brands.

Melanie and I were there in Sequim only earlier this week, this town to which my parents had retreated once all that work was finished. Lavender had been in bloom everywhere.

The news of an amputation was not a surprise. And not a death sentence. This was a terrible thing, Melanie and I both knew and agreed. But it would be for the best. Then I called my mom, and we talked for a while, and we knew and agreed that this was for the best. "The doctor's going to do it Monday morning," she said, "and he says maybe in a week he can go back to the rehab center and get started. The doctor says he's going to feel so much better after this is over," she said, and I'd heard in her voice fear and relief at once.

Now, a day later, fifteen pages of words written and delivered, people I don't know perhaps angry with me, I am walking alone to my hotel in a falling mist.

"This is another essay about the death of a father," I say again.

I say it because, as the editor of a literary journal and as a teacher of writing, I have read a million stories and essays and poems about the death of a father.

I say it because I know I will write these words one day.

But he hasn't yet died. I just know it's coming, as it is for every one of us, and I wonder why I would think the essay I have not written but which I know I one day will might be any different from all those I have read before. Any better. Any more meaningful.

"This is another essay about the death of a father," I say again, still in rhythm with my steps back to the hotel, where I will try to get to sleep at a decent hour because tomorrow I will be traveling yet again, this time to a place very far away.

Then the next words come to me, the ones that let me know it doesn't matter how my story will be different, because it will be. Because it is.

"This is another essay about the death of a father," I say, "but the difference is, this father is mine."

4

I have lived too much with words. I have spent my life trafficking in them. I have spent too much time working them to an end: a story, a novel, an essay. A critique. A lecture. Abstracts, overviews, synopses, blurbs. Letters, e-mails, text messages. Answers and answers and answers. I am too much with words.

On this day, as I try to write down this story, I know more deeply than I ever have the truth of Ecclesiastes 12:12 (NASB): "But beyond this, my son, be warned: the writing of many books is endless, and excessive devotion to books is wearying to the body."

I have worked with words too many years.

As I write this, I am seeing there is no way to write this.

But here is a small piece of paper on my desk, always here with me. A quote from John Berryman: "You should always be trying to write a poem you are unable to write, a poem you lack the technique, the language, the courage to achieve. Otherwise, you're merely repeating yourself, going nowhere because that's always easiest."

Berryman and the Bible. Both true.

There is no way to write this.

5

I keep walking, turn down one street, then another, and I am back at my hotel. I nod at the doorman outside, the bellmen in the lobby, the desk clerk behind the vast marble counter. I ride the elevator up to my floor and walk to my room, zip the card through the lock. Once inside I take off my jacket and tie, sit on the bed, and call Melanie. I tell her the event went well, though I'd felt like an interloper. I ask if she's heard anything else about my dad. I tell her I love her and that I will miss her the next two weeks and that I will call her before I leave for the airport tomorrow morning.

She tells me she knows I did a good job with the speech and that the only news about my dad is that my sister Leslie will be flying up tomorrow from Los Angeles to be there with my mom for the surgery on Monday and then for a few days afterward. She tells me she loves me and will miss me too.

Then I go to bed and try to get to sleep, because tomorrow I am flying from Denver to Newark, then on to Tel Aviv, and though the flight out of Newark will be overnight, I sleep very poorly on planes.

I'm going to Israel to teach in a program sponsored by the State Department, a seminar in Jerusalem on southern literature and culture in the 1950s and 60s (I'll be teaching three stories by Flannery O'Connor) for Israeli teachers of English from around the country. I'll spend the first week planning the seminar with the other American professor, a poet I haven't yet met, and with the State Department English teaching officer, and with the Cultural Programs specialist from the American Center in Jerusalem. The second week we'll spend in ten-hour workdays of seminars and lectures and projects and discussions with the teachers themselves. This will be my second time teaching in the program, and in three months Melanie and I will be moving to Israel for an entire semester, where I will be the visiting writer at a university in Tel Aviv. Part of my job this trip will be to begin looking for an apartment—we want to live in Jerusalem—and to meet somehow with one of the professors from the university.

There is all this to think about as I lie there on a king bed in a dark hotel room in Denver: how much I will miss Melanie, finding a home in Jerusalem, all that work the next two weeks, whether I've divorced myself from fellow believers over the matter of books. And my father.

We were with him just five days before, Melanie and I at the end of our vacation out west. I'd taught at a writer's conference in Salt Lake City, and on the last day Melanie flew out to meet me. The next morning we drove across Utah and Nevada to Incline City on Lake Tahoe to stay with Melanie's aunt and uncle. We spent two days with them, then three days hiking at Yosemite, then took two days driving up to Sequim, where we stayed at my parents' duplex apartment. My older brother Brad and his wife, Joan, live in Sequim too—they were the first to relocate there twenty years ago, Brad a carpenter and the town growing fast with retirees—so we visited with them as well. Tim and Bridget, my younger brother and his wife, live in Sumner, just outside Tacoma, and we spent the Fourth of July with them before flying home to Baton Rouge on Wednesday the fifth. Melanie washed clothes while I spent a few hours at work on Thursday, then headed back home to repack for this trip to Denver and the two weeks in Jerusalem.

We knew the morning we'd driven out of Salt Lake that Dad was in the hospital again with his leg problems. He'd been put on prednisone and had had another bout of vasculitis, a sore on his left leg infected and refusing to heal. Mom kept telling us when we called each evening from the road not to worry, that this was all the same old, same old of his diabetes and its problems, that we'd see them soon enough. So we enjoyed our vacation: staying with Dick and Marilyn in their home perched on the Nevada side of Lake Tahoe, the whole house cantilevered out into its grand view of the lake and the Sierra Nevadas; hiking the six-mile loop up the Merced River from the bottom of the Yosemite Valley past, first, the mist rainbows of Vernal Falls, then on up to the top of Nevada Falls, where the cold and calm river disappears off the cliff edge, dropping 600 feet to the granite rocks below. We'd driven down from the mountains to Modesto, where we climbed on I-5 North, stopping at The Olive Pit in Corning to buy jars of almond- and garlic- and blue cheese–stuffed olives. At dusk we stopped in Roseburg, Oregon, at an Elmer's Restaurant just over the South Umpqua River and had pancakes for dinner, then headed on in the dark to a hotel in Eugene.

The next morning we got up early, and drove 340 miles straight to the parking lot of Olympic Memorial Hospital in Port Angeles, Washington.

We walked into my dad's room to see him sitting up on the edge of the bed while a nurse hovered beside him, adjusting him this way and that to help him swing his legs off the edge. My mom was there with him, and when she saw us she hugged us and hugged us. "We're so happy you made it," she said, and my dad grunted out, "You made it."

His legs were wrapped in Ace bandages, dark spots here and there where whatever toxins in him were seeping out. My mom had warned us.

She'd warned us as well that he wasn't too alert and that he wasn't talking much. But he seemed better than she'd made out each time we'd checked in with her while we were on the road. Here he was in a pair of shorts and a hooded zip-up sweatshirt, moving around, words out of him as soon as he'd seen us. His eyes were sharp. And the wraps on his legs weren't as bad as I'd thought they'd be, either. Just those dark spots here and there.

"He's doing a whole lot better," my mom said once the hugging was over and the nurse was gone. "They're letting him move out of here and into the rehab center back in Sequim tomorrow so they can get him up and walking again," she said, and held her hands together in front of her, smiling with her head tilted just the smallest way. Not a real smile. One of those smiles I knew she gave when she wanted us to know she wasn't happy.

A sad smile. That's what I'm trying to describe as I write this.

"Going to get some coffee," my dad said, and here came the nurse back into the room pushing a wheelchair.

"The doctor says he can have a cup of coffee down in the cafeteria," my mom said, and looked at us. Here now was a real smile. "He said we can go outside and take him for a walk, too."

The nurse knelt and slipped wool socks on his feet, then she and my mom pulled a pair of sweatpants up over his feet and legs, and now my dad was standing in the room, one hand on the edge of the bed to steady him, and the nurse eased the wheelchair in behind him as he turned and slowly sat down.

"Coffee," I said. "That's good news," and I moved to where the nurse stood ready to push him in the wheelchair. I said, "I'll do that," and nodded at her, a pale woman with short blond hair frizzed out and wearing one of those colorful balloons-on-strings scrubs outfits. She smiled, nodded at me, then left the room.

I pushed him on out, my mom leading the way, Melanie beside her.

Do not here think me some kind of good guy for taking the wheelchair and pushing my dad down to the cafeteria for a cup of coffee. Do not look at me in this moment as the thoughtful son doing the right thing in relieving the nurse or keeping my mom from the work of pushing that chair. Instead, look at my father, and my mother, and my wife, and the view of the Strait of Juan de Fuca through the huge picture windows there in the hospital cafeteria as we slowly wheel into the room. Look at the brilliant deep blue of the water down below the bluffs this hospital sits upon, and past that blue the dark green edge of Canada a few miles away, the small and worriless chunk of white ferryboat far out there and headed across.

Don't look at me, because all I wanted was to have something to do. To stand behind and to push and to think only on this smallest of jobs. I wanted something to do with my hands. I wanted to work.

I wanted to get out of the way.

6

I write the way I do and about whom I do because of Raymond Carver. When I read his story collection *What We Talk About When We Talk About Love,* I was a grad student at UMass Amherst in desperate need of a comeuppance. I thought writing was all about the author, that this was some sort of show about me, and how wonderfully adept I could be at juggling words. I thought my job was to give metaphor to everything at hand, and thereby to inspire a kind of awe in a reader at how creative I was.

I was twenty-three. This was 1981, me just out of Cal State

Long Beach with a BA and an idea I wanted to be a writer, and an idea, too, of what a writer was: a glittering magician.

That first semester at UMass, my stories were promptly destroyed in workshop. No holds barred. It seemed as if everyone in class, from the professor to fellow newcomers, had agreed beforehand to play dog-pile on Bret. The sore fact, though, is that I deserved it. To this day, I do not understand how I even got into the program.

Then, over winter break, I read *What We Talk About When We Talk About Love*.

Although his next collection, *Cathedral*, would become my favorite of all his books, reading *What We Talk About When We Talk About Love* changed my life. I saw, suddenly and fully, that a story was about the people involved. I saw that embellishment brought to the table an unwanted intruder: the author. I saw that people, in the dire straits we all of us have known and will know, carried with them their own ragged and sorrowful and mysterious worth. I saw that too many words about people made those same people smaller. And I saw that working people, the same people I'd known all my life, were important in and of themselves, and mattered.

Back then none of us knew any of the editorial tumult Gordon Lish had put Raymond Carver through, tumult that has only come fully to light in the last few years, and knowing now what I did not know then of how these stories came to be in no way blunts or explodes or skews the genuine revelation about the art of writing that came to me through Carver's work.

What I saw in his work was that in my own, I had to be the last one heard from in this pile of words I was arranging, and that humility was the most valuable tool I could have, because the people about whom I wanted to write mattered so very much more than the paltry desires of the writer himself. They mattered so very much more than me. My job was to get out of the way.

Raymond Carver taught me all of those things, simply by having written his own stories and my then reading them at the exact moment I needed to have read them. I worked with great teachers—John Hermann at Cal State, Tamas Aczel and Jay Neugeboren and James Baldwin at UMass—but the best teacher I had was Raymond Carver, and those stories.

After reading them, I threw away everything I had written to that point and began, only then, to write.

I met Mr. Carver twice, the first time after a reading at the University of New Hampshire in October, 1982, not even a year after I'd had my first encounter with his work. Melanie and I, along with Betsy Adams, one of Melanie's fellow administrative assistants in the psychology department at UMass, made the three-hour drive up from Amherst to Durham. I'd tried to mobilize as many MFA students as I could to go hear him, but no one was interested; the only person from the program who showed any interest at all was the poet Madeline DeFrees, the tiny and white-haired and iron-strong interim director of the program, who'd told me she was an old friend of his from their days out west. Of course I'd been in awe at this—I'd come to her office to express my consternation at how no students wanted to go see the best writer I'd ever read and ended up meeting someone who knew him as a friend—and though she shared my confusion at why no one wanted to go, she also told me to say hello to him for her, and I knew then that I had my in, the reason I might have to meet him, if the evening came to that: I would be allowed to meet Raymond Carver because I had a message from a friend.

We arrived at the reading at UNH to find the only empty seats left were in the last row of what looked like a math lecture hall, with its tiered rows and huge chalkboard behind a podium, and just as we sat down, some guy named Charles Simic stepped to the podium and introduced him, and then I listened to Raymond Carver read "Preservation."

He was quiet but confident, humble but certain of these words he was speaking. He simply read the story, pausing now and again for the smallest effects, and to look up at the audience as though to make sure we were listening.

After he read, Mr. Simic announced that there would be a reception for anyone who wanted to come, and as I write this I am in a kind of awe about the audacity and ambition and desire I was filled with back then, because we three people from 250 miles away, no relation whatsoever to anyone at all from UNH, simply followed the crowd to another building, a kind of gathering place for such events on campus that seemed more like someone's house than anything official, and started to mingle.

Here he was in the room, talking to people, a glass of what we knew had to be ice water in his hand. He smiled, nodded, spoke, laughed, sipped at the water. Right there. And then there came a moment when he was suddenly alone, and Melanie nudged me the last few feet toward him—we'd lost Betsy somewhere in the room—and now my wife and I were standing with Raymond Carver.

"Madeline DeFrees says hello," I said, and he smiled wide, nodded, said, "She's been a friend for a long time."

Here I was, talking to Raymond Carver.

He had salt-and-pepper hair, and he was humble when I told him how great the reading was and how important he was to me. I asked him if he'd ever before written a story about a writer, and he had to think about it, and he said that, yes, there was the story "Put Yourself In My Shoes," but that he didn't much like writing about writers, because there were more important things to write about. What mattered was making the rent, he said, and putting food on the table, and paying the electric bill.

It was an answer I had wanted to hear, because I had come to believe, through his work and my own life as well, the same thing: working people matter most.

We talked more—I was standing with my wife and talking to Raymond Carver, just we three!—and then I asked him if he would think about coming to UMass to give a reading, though I had no idea about how these things happened and owned no authority whatsoever to have asked. He said yes, he would love to, and that he was friends with Jim Tate too, the other poet teaching in the program at UMass. It would be great to see Madeline and Jim both.

Then, with an even grander audacity than asking him to come give a reading, an impertinence I look back and shake my head at to this day, there came to me the sudden and heavy hand of ignorance and ambition both, and I asked him, "Can I send you some of my stories?"

"Sure," he said, and smiled again. "Send me two or three in a few months. Send them to the English department at Syracuse."

I could not believe—do not now believe, either—his good will toward me, and my ambition, though he had taught me that to be a writer is to be humble. That to be a writer means to get oneself out of the way.

A few months later, I'd gone on in my audacious way and sent him two stories. He wrote back a very gracious if barely legible one-page letter about how much he enjoyed the stories and how he thought I was on the right track. He also mentioned he was sorry he wouldn't be able to use either of them for an upcoming *Ploughshares* issue he was editing and how hard it was having to put together the issue and knowing so many promising young writers as he did and having to say no to most all of them. Somehow he had gotten in his mind that I had sent them to him for *Ploughshares*, a mistake that didn't bother me at all; what mattered was that Raymond Carver had read my stories; he'd written me a letter!

The second time I met him was a year and a half later, when he read at Harvard to celebrate the publication of that issue of *Ploughshares*. Melanie hadn't been with me this time, she at home in Northampton in our second-floor apartment on Walnut Street with our baby, Zebulun, nine months old by then. But I'd finally found a Carverite at UMass, Jim Brace-Thompson, a fellow MFA student who'd been happy to go with me. We'd met a year or so before at a student reading in another student's apartment, one Dorothea Barrett, a larger-than-life fiction writer from England who wore tank T-shirts and didn't shave her pits. I'd seen Jim around before, knew he was a fiction writer too, and decided to introduce myself. He had a pack of Gauloises, and we sat and smoked a couple of them there on the ratty couch Dorothea had. I didn't smoke as a rule but puffed my way through mine because I thought the pack was cool, that bright ice blue. We'd talked about who we liked to read—he was a huge fan of some new writer named Michael Martone, nobody I'd ever heard of—and then our talk had turned to Raymond Carver.

Once we were through with the cigarettes, he told me not to tell his wife he smoked; I told him not to tell mine I'd even tried them. Thus we were friends, and here we were a year later, driving out the Mass Pike and on into Cambridge. It was raining, I remember.

Mr. Carver read "Cathedral" to a lecture hall even more packed than the one at UNH had been—people stood along the walls—and I will not forget his looking at the audience and saying the single word "Bub" in the narrator's deadpan voice, the entire hall filling with laughter. Nor will I forget the giant reception afterward, this time in some poorly lit, warehouse-like space. I won't forget it, because when I made my way to him and introduced myself again, he remembered me, then introduced me to Tess Gallagher, told me to give Madeline and Jim his best, and signed my copy of *Cathedral*.

He remembered me.

Then I got to give him my news, an entrée that didn't depend upon word from Madeline or anyone else: since he'd read those two stories I'd sent him, one had been accepted by the *Iowa Review*, the other by the *Yale Review,* and I had him to thank for having been an encouragement to me for his simply having read them. He congratulated me heartily, shook my hand, patted me on the back, smiling all the while, and then the crowd had pressed in and in, and the meeting was over, ahead of Jim Brace-Thompson and me the long and wet ride home from Cambridge to Amherst.

Life

But I had talked with Mr. Carver. He'd remembered me, this man who wrote about people who had to make the rent and put food on the table, here celebrated at Harvard.

I have gone on to publish thirteen books, all of them in one way or another about working people: soda pop salesmen, secretaries, janitors, computer programmers, cashiers, housewives, firemen, plumbers—and I am not ashamed to say that my first two novels and the first two collections of stories sound a great deal like Raymond Carver. And though I don't write anything like him anymore, that same precision of his, that same sharp and spare voice, and the same careful eye he had for the people about whom he wrote, still inform me.

I am still trying to get me out of the way.

One of those books, the seventh, is about my father, and my sons, and my brothers. A book of nonfiction, a series of essays written to keep from passing away the days I was living through back then, when I saw my two young sons doing the same stupid things to each other that my two brothers and I had done to each other growing up. The same stupid things, too, that I'd heard stories of my father and his two brothers doing to each other.

With that book, I'd wanted to catch something in the words I was putting together that would hold still for a moment those moments themselves. My two sons—Zebulun, the older, and Jacob, the younger—are most featured in the essays, the two of them around nine and seven when the book ends.

Zeb is now twenty-five and married. He's in the army, a cavalry scout, and served in Iraq from September 2006 to November 2007. Maggie, the woman he married, is the same girl he took to the prom when he was a sophomore in high school, Maggie then a freshman.

Jacob is twenty-three and lives and works in Alexandria, Virginia, for a nonprofit trade organization that helps get food from one place in the world to another. He drives a car he spends too much money on but that brings him a kind of joy I don't understand. He's named the car Veronica.

But in that book, every time I open it, they are only boys. The last I see of them inside those words I trafficked in to try and hold them still, they are two kids, nine and seven.

I am a kid in there, too, as are my own brothers, all of us the sons of Wilman Sequoia Lott. We fight with each other, betray each other, make up and ignore and love each other. We are always young inside that book, none of us ever any older than at its end, when Brad, Tim, and I are in our thirties and working inside the unfinished story of our lives.

And of course my father is there too.

In the book he is always at work—for Nehi, for RC Cola, for the food brokerage—and always showing us, his children, the importance of doing our best, and the proof of that labor: his provision for our family.

So is it at all a surprise that the first book I ever wrote, my first novel, was about an RC Cola salesman who finds a kind of solace in his work, and that throughout all I have written there runs a thread of salesmen, and cashiers at grocery stores, and firemen and plumbers and work and work and work?

This is how I only see now, as I write this one morning almost three years after my father has died, the first way in which the lives of Raymond Carver and my father intersect: this fact of work, of its first importance.

And this is how I count Mr. Carver, though I met him only twice, though he read so little of my work, and though my life only touched his in the smallest and most tangential way, a kind of father too.

7

For no good reason other than that I have slept in after yesterday's work of writing that lecture for the book award dinner and then delivering it, and because I have forgotten how far out of Denver the airport is—33 miles from downtown—I am late for my flight. I am supposed to be there at least two hours in advance because this is an international flight, and I am a cliché: I rush into the airport at noon, my flight leaving in thirty minutes, and at the kiosk out front of the counter I flag down an agent and let her know I am here, that I am running late, that I am going to Tel Aviv through Newark, and here is my bag to check through, and am I going to make this plane, and will my bag make it too?

She looks at me and shakes her head, lets out a gruff sigh as she slaps the tag onto my bag, and then we are hustling past the long line at security, the woman telling me over her shoulder as we pass all these people dutifully on time for their flights what I already know: "You're supposed to be here at least two hours in advance of an international flight." I only say "I'm sorry" three or four times and "I forgot how far out the airport is here," as though any of this will make anything better, and here we are at security, and I turn to thank her as I set down my briefcase and small green backpack to pull out my passport, but she is already gone.

I make the flight, and because I have traveled enough miles with the carrier, I have been given a business-class upgrade for this leg to Newark, and I sit down, finally, tired already though I have slept in. Tired already, though I am only at the beginning of a very long travel day.

I am given a small bowl of warm mixed nuts by the smiling attendant, and then the gin and tonic I requested when she'd asked, and before I can finish either one, the door to the jetway is closed, the bowl and drink taken up, and we begin.

I haven't called Melanie yet to see about my dad, the morning has been so rushed. But also because there is a piece of me that doesn't want whatever news it is she might have for me. I am thinking instead about the night before, and the talk I gave, and the people who came up and thanked me and those who didn't, and the words I spoke out loud to myself as I'd walked back to my hotel.

And then I cannot help but think, as we rise up off the flat plain and head east and east and east this bright summer day, of having been there only five days before.

Once we finished our coffee, the four of us sitting at a table beside the hospital cafeteria's huge windows and looking out on sea and sky, we decided it was time to take that walk outside. The doctor had okayed this, my mother told us—my father was getting better, and would be checked out tomorrow, brought to the rehab center in Sequim to start working on strengthening his legs but the real reason we were going to take a walk is that my dad wanted outside.

I'd watched him some as we talked over coffee. He was clean-shaven, his hair combed. He was squinting for all that light in on us and held the Styrofoam cup with both hands in his lap, his elbows on the arms of the wheelchair. I could see on his hands deep blue bruises beneath the old-man skin, bruises that were always there because of his diabetes, I knew, and I wondered every time if they were at all painful. But I didn't ask.

He spoke now and again, about the nurses being so good to him, about this coffee being the first cup he'd had since he'd been checked in two weeks ago, about not wanting to go to that damned rehab center, that he could work things out at home.

Then he said, "Let's go," and looked around, set his eyes upon the doorway we'd come through to get here, and we left.

He was getting better, I could tell. It was in the way he'd said it, the cranky authority inside those two words.

We walked along one hallway and another, my mom and Melanie ahead of us, Mom leading the way, me still pushing the wheelchair, and suddenly we were at two sliding doors that quietly opened for us, then outside.

I could smell the ocean, feel the eddy of wind from across it there in front of the hospital, and we turned left, followed a long sidewalk beside the parking lot onto a painted sweeping arc of a crosswalk that led out to the street. We walked fifty yards or so down a concrete sidewalk away from the hospital, houses to our left, the street with its cars moving too fast on our right, my mother talking and talking, the cool wind picking even harder at us now. Then we turned left down a street that dead-ended a hundred yards away, we could see, on a view to the water.

Once there, we all only looked out on it: the water, the land far away, the sky above it all. Though it was late afternoon by this time, the sun was still high and sharp—early July in the Pacific Northwest—so that when the wind eased for a moment I could feel the heat of it on my bare arms and on my face.

There was in these few moments on a bluff in Port Angeles, Washington, a kind of peace to everything, though I do not want to give the moment some sheen of significance it did not have. My father only sat in his wheelchair with me behind him, my mom and my wife beside us. This was the first time my father had been outside in two weeks, and we watched the ocean, felt the sun, smelled the wind.

Then the wind came straight and sharp off the water at us, and I was cold, and Melanie was too, her arms crossed, her shoulders up, the wind in her hair.

"Should we go in?" I said. "It's cold out here," and I looked at my dad there in the chair in front of me, me still holding the handles.

He didn't move, just looked out on the water.

"We probably should," my mom said, "but it's so nice out here."

Then we turned, headed back to the hospital and the warmth in there.

Once back in his room, my dad stood from the chair, put his hand on the edge of the bed. He turned around and, giving out now and again a hard grunt and grimacing all the while, he leaned against the bed and slowly eased back, lifting first one leg and then the other.

I still stood at the chair, watched while my mom held one of his arms, Melanie at the foot of the bed, neither of us knowing what to do here.

And then, just before he got his second leg up on the bed, he stopped, exasperated, I could tell from these grunts, at what I figured had to be the work of all this.

He looked up at me. His eyes were open wide, his eyebrows high on his forehead, and now it seemed he was surprised somehow, perhaps even angry. Or just tired of everything.

But he paused there in the work of getting back into bed and said, "I know I've done wrong things, but I know I've been forgiven. That's it."

It came from nowhere I could figure. Maybe it was something my mom was talking about—she talks sometimes simply to be heard, and sometimes I just stop listening—or maybe it was the end of a conversation the two of them had been having before Melanie and I had even entered the hospital.

But he said it, looking at me. He glanced next to Melanie, then back to me, and then the moment was over. He continued easing back, my mom attending him, and into bed.

We said nothing.

That evening, once we'd followed Mom from the hospital back to Sequim and their duplex and dropped off our bags, we took her out to dinner at The Three Crabs. She talked on the way there about how she and Dad had eaten there only a couple of times, years ago, but that the view was beautiful, you could see Dungeness Spit and the lighthouse out at the end if you got a table beside the windows. At one point we passed a carved wooden sign on the right for one of the lavender farms out there, Jardin du Soleil, and she went on about how of course it was a shame we didn't come a week later when we would've been here for the Lavender Festival, but this was when our vacation was and we couldn't help it, she understood entirely. But we should definitely think about stopping in at one of the lavender farms before we left town, because this was the peak, right now, and it was all so beautiful, and Jardin du Soleil, well, that one was just the best, just the best.

We kept driving, and pulled off the road onto a smaller one that led across the wide marsh flats north of town. Mom was going to have the crab cakes, of course, and she was glad to get away from being at the hospital, though not glad, of course, to be away from your father. She'd been there these two weeks, and through his in and out in and out before that, and she warned him about those sores on his legs but, no, he wouldn't listen to her and refused to do anything about them until he could barely walk on them and the sores were oozing nonstop, sorry to be talking about such ugly things.

The restaurant was an old square building, the parking lot what had to have been a beach at one time, and we parked. In front of us lay Dungeness Bay, and, yes, we could see the spit off to the left, that thin run of land across the water, the tiny knob of a building out on it that was the lighthouse. The sun was finally on its way down, though there was still plenty of light left.

She seemed happier at dinner and continued talking: about the physical therapist they had been to see whose office was in her own house, and how she massaged his legs and wrapped them with these towels my mom was certain hadn't been washed, and how dirty the woman's house had been, cat hair everywhere and the whole place smelling weird, and how the therapist was just some strange hippie-like character; about the rehab center and how one friend of hers thought it wasn't a good place to go to, but that another said her husband had gone through physical therapy for his broken hip there and had gotten great care.

"He doesn't want to go in there," she said. "He's afraid of going in there, because he thinks that's the last place he's going to be. He thinks he's just going into a rest home, and that'll be that."

Melanie and I put in now and again whatever we thought might help—the hospital staff seemed nice, it must have been good for

Dad to get outside of the hospital, they wouldn't be putting him in a rehab center if they didn't think he was going to get better—but Mom's talk was about all of what she had been through and Dad too and how glad she was we were here, and how we'd go to Brad and Joan's tonight for a minute and then back to the duplex, you two must be tired from all you've done today, and I love the crab cakes—Dungeness crab cakes—they serve here.

But I could see in the same patter she always gave something else, a pall of sadness over everything, and of fatigue too, for how much work it had to be simply to stand watch at a hospital, to get up and drive the half hour or so from Sequim to Port Angeles knowing what was at the end of the ride, then back home at night and knowing what was at the end of that ride too.

"If you just could have come out here next week," she said yet again, as though her words might have changed anything at all, "you could have been here for the Lavender Festival."

We had the Dungeness crab cakes.

8

Why do I have to work with words? Why is it they have fallen to me, so that I am the one who has to put in this manner these words, the responsibility mine? Why is it the work of recording these events is *my* work, and why did a sentence form in my head while walking a street in Denver even before the event had come about, and why is it I knew even then that I would be writing these words, here, this moment, about his death?

My older brother, Brad, is a finish carpenter. My younger brother, Tim, is a Fritos salesman. My sister, Leslie, takes care of her family. We all have the same parents, were all raised in the same household.

So why am I the one to have been given words as my work, and given the words *This is another essay about the death of a father,* when fathers die all the time, and people write of their dead fathers all the time, and there is no end to dead fathers and people writing of them?

He was my brothers' father, too. He was my sister's father, too. I am so tired of words.

In the book about him and my brothers and my sons, my father is always at work, but he is, I see, teaching us about work as well. He is bringing us sons along with him Saturday mornings to stock the shelves of the grocery stores on his route in Long Beach, California, we three a trail behind him of awed boys amidst the wonder and mystery of backrooms piled high with cases of bottles, boxes of toilet paper and soup, waxed cardboard cartons of lettuce and tomatoes. We are boys witnessing our father at work as he stacks cases of bottles in that backroom, then wheels them on a hand truck through metal saloon doors out into the bright surprise of light on the grocery store aisles, and if he so decides to bless us, we are boys allowed to help him stock those shelves, then clean up the bottles with the feather duster he has drawn from his back pocket for just this moment.

And we are boys on other Saturday mornings bent to the work of pulling weeds along the backyard fence in Buena Park, while he pushes a mower, stopping now and again to point out what blades and stems we have missed; or we are sweeping broken glass from the asphalt lots of the RC Cola plant in South Phoenix all summer long, ready at any moment for him to come out onto the lot from his office inside and instruct us on how to *push* a push broom and not *pull* it; or we are over for barbequed steaks at the house in Huntington Beach on Sunday afternoons once we have all three moved out, and we are suffering through the rigors of a meal in which our jobs at RC are reconnoitered—I am a salesman, Tim is a driver, Brad is on the table-set crew—and all things Work are pored over, and over again.

But in the book he is also a child in backwoods Mississippi being harassed by an older brother who knows just how far my dad can throw a rock so that my uncle never gets hit by him. He's a teenager with a girl beside him in the cab of his father's truck, suavely putting his arm on the seatback as he looks out the rear window, the move a calculated event to get his arm around the girl. But when my dad gives it the gas, the truck's rear wheels slip off the road in the Mississippi woods and down an embankment; panicked, he guns the engine, and the truck slides even faster down the embankment, then rolls once, then again, before settling right-side up at the bottom of the drainage ditch, the girl still sitting there beside him.

And my dad is a young man hosing out a garage on a Saturday morning back in Buena Park, while we three sons run as fast as we can from bright sunlight on the asphalt driveway into that dark garage with its slick cement floor, all of us sliding barefoot as far as we can. My dad seems to smile at this, though we can fall and sometimes do smack onto that wet cement, a fact that does not stop either his hosing out the garage or we boys from running back out to the driveway, turning around, and trying it again.

In that moment in the book he is always that young man, seeming to smile.

But near the end of the book are the following words, meant as summary of the lives we sons and our father are leading inside a book that will always be occurring only in the moment it has tried to capture: "It ends with no end at all, of course, as we are all still alive, still here."

The sentence is a lie. My father is no longer alive.

But the sentence is also the truth. He's here, and he is working, and working.

He *is* my brothers' father. He *is* my sister's father. So why, when words are so deceitful, so scheming as to speak truth and untruth in the very same instant, am I the one to have these untrustworthy things before me, and why is the work of putting them in the correct order my work and mine only?

Life

The answer, I know, no matter how tired I am or how deceitful words may be, is so simple as to make the asking a stupid act: Because this is the work I have been given.

9

I have two letters from Mr. Carver—the one about those stories I'd sent him, the other about that possible reading at UMass, an event that never happened—and I have as well a Polaroid photo, taken by Tess Gallagher, of him and Madeline DeFrees standing in the living room of Ms. Gallagher's home in Port Angeles, Washington. The photo was given to me by Madeline after a visit she'd made the summer of 1983, when I was entering my last year as a student in the MFA program, my meeting him at Harvard almost a year away. Madeline told me when she returned from the trip that while visiting them she had mentioned me, told them about this young man in the program who was such an admirer of Carver's stories and had seen him read at UNH, and that Ray—she called him Ray—remembered me for having sent him my stories, and that nervy invitation to come read.

He'd remembered me.

Ms. Gallagher had then taken a picture of Madeline and Mr. Carver to be given to me. In it, he wears glasses and stands in a gray flannel shirt, Madeline beside him and at least a foot shorter and wearing a white blouse and her big glasses, the two of them smiling.

I also have a postcard from him, upon which he declined in heartfelt and again nearly illegible words to read the galleys of my first novel, *The Man Who Owned Vermont*, a begging off that also included a request to have my editor send him a copy when it came out. I remember being disappointed, and actually a little put off, by the response. Not so much for his saying no, but at his asking for a free book in the same small square of paper.

I keep the letters, photo, and postcard tucked into my copy of John Gardner's *On Becoming a Novelist*, the book a gift from Carver via Madeline from that same trip in 1983. He gave it to Madeline to give to me from his stash of author's copies—he'd written the foreword—and I've read the book at least a dozen times, require its reading for any student who comes into any class I ever teach.

And I also keep tucked in there a copy of Carver's obituary from the *New York Times*, his death a surprise to me, my discovery of it mired in my own ego.

We were living here in Charleston by then, and though I'd heard from Madeline over the prior year about Carver's cancer, I'd also heard he was getting better somehow, that perhaps he would make it through.

My second novel, *A Stranger's House*, was published in August 1988, and word came down to me from Paul Slovak, my publicist at Viking, that a review in the daily *New York Times* was about to appear, but no exact date could be given. So each morning I headed out early to the closest place I knew that sold the paper, the Harris-Teeter grocery store three miles away, and bought a copy, then sat in the car and tore through it in search of word about Me.

And I found one morning on the book page a thick black square two columns wide, inside it the words "In Memoriam, Raymond Carver, 1938–1988."

I hadn't even known. I'd not seen the obituary the day before because I'd been looking only for a review about my book, but this black-bordered square with its terrible news was too big for my ego to miss.

Raymond Carver had died. And I was worried about a review.

I called Madeline that evening. She told me Carver had found out earlier in the summer that the cancer was back, that no one was to be told, that he wanted to die quietly and without fanfare.

I hadn't known him, hadn't been a student of his or anything near it. Twice I'd been one among the crowd who'd been there to appreciate his work, and though at a couple of moments he'd remembered me, he had to have remembered a million people for the reasons all of us remember those we do. I had no claim to him other than a few pieces of paper, a Polaroid, a book given as a gift through a third party.

He was gone, and I knew then a strange sort of loss, a loss of something at once close and remote. I'd lost something I never had, but felt the loss all the same.

A few months later I was at work on the next novel, a big sprawling thing I had no idea how to write because it was so big. But I was writing it. The story was about a woman in Mississippi, the mother of five children with the sixth on the way, the children born in a log cabin her husband had built. It was a story I'd grown up with, the woman my grandmother, one of the children my father, the rest my aunts and uncles. But one morning as I was writing of the woman's childhood, living inside the dream that a story is, there suddenly appeared at her back door a black girl, someone who would, over the course of the novel, become the lifelong friend of the narrator.

I needed a name for her. She was standing outside a screen door, the narrator inside the kitchen and looking out at her, and of course they were friends, and of course she knew what this girl standing out there was named. But *I* didn't know her name, and so I listened.

Cathedral, I heard. *Her name is Cathedral.*

There was never any argument at all in me. This was her name. Cathedral, the lifelong friend of the novel's narrator, a woman whose own name was Jewel.

Cathedral. A name suddenly given me to honor Raymond Carver, and to say, in my own way, thank you.

Nine years later, in 1997, I would be asked to teach at a writer's conference in Port Townsend, Washington, out on the Olympic Peninsula. I'd never been to the Northwest before, and the conference was known to be one of the best in the country, set at Fort Worden and looking out onto Puget Sound and the Strait of Juan de Fuca. Brad and Joan lived with their two daughters in Sequim, a little town only thirty miles away. They'd been there for the last ten years or so, Brad working as a carpenter helping build retirement homes, but I'd never visited them up there. I went.

I took a late-evening shuttle from Sea-Tac, so I saw nothing of the land on the two-and-a-half-hour drive in to Fort Worden, only taillights and headlights, the strata of lights on the hills and through the trees. Lights that began to thin only once we crossed the Tacoma Narrows Bridge, nearly giving up entirely once we crossed next the Hood Canal Bridge, until we approached Port Townsend and the lights of its paper mill. Then here I was, delivered to the door of an old barracks building, my rooms the bottom floor, the apartment cold and cavernous but the bed soft and waiting.

I awoke to a landscape alien and beautiful at once: mountains everywhere, cool crisp air, light of a different quality than I had ever known. The sky stayed lit until late at night, the sun high and sharp all day long, we were so far north. And there were good people there, faculty and staff and students alike. I held my classes outside, the students seated around a picnic table, our view there on the old parade grounds one that looked out onto the Strait of Juan de Fuca. A beautiful view, a word that seems empty as I write it for how beautiful the water and sky and mountains all were.

I'd never been here before.

We were given a free day in the middle of the conference, and I met Brad for breakfast at the Bayview Restaurant in town, a place with tables next to huge windows that look out onto the water, ferries pulling in and out of the pier and heading for places I didn't know. I hadn't seen Brad in four and a half years, not since a gigantic Christmas at out parents' house in Huntington Beach when my mother insisted the entire family—four children, four spouses, and all eight grandchildren—spend the night of Christmas Eve together so we could all wake up the next morning for the extravaganza. Brad and I talked over breakfast about the house he was building by himself and how long it was taking, about Fort Worden and how his daughters, my nieces—Alyson, eleven, and Rachel, nine—had been there for field trips before and loved the beach and the old buildings and the parade grounds, and about how hard it was to be living in that trailer parked on their lot, the four of them relegated to a space for the last three years that he could hitch to the back of a truck and pull away.

Then we drove on over to Sequim, to see Joan and Alyson and Rachel, to see the house, to see that trailer. And though I wanted to do all this, spend time with my family, let Brad cook dinner for me—he was and remains famous for his skills at barbequing—I also had another reason to go over to Sequim.

The next town beyond it was Port Angeles, where Raymond Carver was buried.

At some point on our drive out of Port Townsend on a two-lane road that skirted the edge of Discovery Bay, passed the 7 Cedars Casino at the bottom of Sequim Bay, and broadened out, finally, onto the level ground of Sequim, with its mix of old-fashioned Main Street and bright new duplexes, strip malls, and old wooden barns, I asked him if we might also drive over to Port Angeles and a place called Ocean View Cemetery to visit the grave of this writer who meant so much to me.

He knew where it was, the cemetery beyond the dump at the far end of town, from having to haul junk from building sites now and again. After a barbeque of sausages and steaks out front of his trailer—a vacation trailer maybe 20 feet long, bunk beds at one end, at the other a bunk above a banquette, along one side a couch wide enough to sleep one person, across from that a stove and a mini-fridge; a hovel they'd been living in for three years and that would make me cry when I called Melanie later that night and told her how small it was and how long they'd been living in it while work on the house crept along—and after I'd treated Alyson and Rachel and Brad and Joan to dessert at a frozen yogurt shop in one of those strip malls in town, Brad took me out there.

It seemed very far away, though the drive took only a half hour or so, most of it along a wide highway—US 101—that dipped and curved and leveled out and curved again as it headed into the town itself. The Olympic Range was always to our left, the water off to our right, and here was Port Angeles: somewhat congested, somewhat industrial, somewhat beat up. We passed through light after light and along business after business, and here stood yet another paper mill, this one on a spit of land that poked out into the strait. We followed the highway as it narrowed at the far end of town and turned off into what seemed a residential area, then into more trees, and now Brad pulled to the right into a narrow driveway, and so into Ocean View Cemetery.

A flat expanse of ground, thick with grass and edged with trees. Here and there stood upright gravestones, but most all of them set flat on the ground. Flowers around, plastic ones and real ones. All this.

And the view.

One whole side of the cemetery was open to the strait, the grounds built on a bluff that overlooked that deep blue water and the sharp green edge of Canada, above it all a sky huge and blue. Trees grew up from the bluff and at the very edge of the grounds, but not in a way that blocked anything. Instead, they only framed and accented the beauty—that empty word again—of the view here.

Brad drove slowly along the narrow gravel lane through the cemetery. Neither of us had been here before, and Brad had never heard of Raymond Carver. There was no one at the cemetery, no sexton with a backhoe or funeral director setting up chairs so that I might ask where the grave was.

But I saw now out Brad's window a low black granite bench—nothing more than a thick elevated slab—with flowers beside it, and as we came closer I could see as well two full-size gravestones flat on the ground, some sort of upright metal arch a couple feet tall to one side of it all.

Life

This would be it, I figured, for no other reason than the austerity of it—a black bench, flat black stones.

Brad eased over a little onto the grass and stopped. We climbed out, and he asked if I was sure this was it, said that the cemetery was a beautiful spot, that he'd been back on this road a hundred times to go to the dump and had never seen the place.

"I'm pretty certain this is it," I said.

We walked across the grass to the bench, and I saw now that beneath one end of it sat a black metal lockbox of sorts, almost a kind of tackle box. In front of the bench lay those two black granite slabs big as tables, between them a narrower slab the same length. The gravestone on the left was inscribed with Carver's name and birth and death dates, the line "Poet, Short Story Writer, Essayist," and beneath it the poem "Late Fragment." On the narrower stone beside it was inscribed the poem "Gravy," both poems written in his last days. Above the poem was an imbedded oval photograph of Carver and Tess Gallagher. To the right of that narrower slab was the other full-sized stone, Ms. Gallagher's name inscribed at the top. At the head of it all stood that metal arch, hanging from it a wind chime.

"Nice place to get buried," Brad said, and I turned to him, saw he was looking out at the water.

I sat down then on the bench and realized, of course, the obvious: anyone sitting here had no choice but to take in this view.

"Yes it is," I said.

I looked back to the gravestones, then leaned over, looked at that metal box. There was no lock on it, only a metal clasp, and I opened it.

Inside was a small notepad and pen in a Ziploc bag.

I opened the bag, looked at the pages: letters and notes and thoughts from people. Ms. Gallagher had written in there, too, only a few days before.

I looked up at the view again, and saw my brother still looking too. He'd lit a cigarette, and he took a drag. Smoke whisked away from him on the breeze out here.

I wrote some things to Ms. Gallagher, about how Mr. Carver had read two stories of mine when I was young.

10

After the crab cakes, Mom and Melanie and I drove over to Brad and Joan's house to visit a few minutes—Brad had finished building their home eight years ago, the trailer a distant bad dream—and we talked for a while about how good Dad looked today, how much he'd improved in the last week or so, the rehab center he'd be check-ing into the next day. We talked about how neither Brad nor Joan needed to help move him over there, that Melanie and Mom and I would do it, bring in the extra TV from Mom and Dad's house, and his clothes, pictures to put on the dresser and hang on the walls in there for however long it would take him to get better.

Then we went back to Mom and Dad's duplex, Melanie and I nearly passing out as our heads hit the pillows for how long this day had been, with its drive straight from Eugene to the hospital, then all this visiting.

The next morning we drove again over to Port Angeles and the hospital, in the hatchback of our rental car the television from their bedroom, a carry-on-sized suitcase with some clothes, a small card-board box with pictures. Dad was already up, ready to go: he wanted out of here, even if it meant he was checking into a place he didn't want to consider, this rehab center a rest home by his measure.

Yet again there was in our driving him back to Sequim a kind of sadness, though *sadness* is, as with other words I have found want-ing in trying to find the language to tell this all, a word that doesn't give me what I want. There was a sadness, yes, but an *other* feeling to it as well, this *other* a kind of beauty, a form of it.

He sat beside me in the front seat, Melanie and Mom behind us. His legs were freshly wrapped, and he had on the sweatshirt and

sweatpants he'd worn the day before, when we'd taken him for coffee and then to the end of the street and the few minutes looking at
the water. It was a bright day, the sun out in its July fullness, the
temperature in the low seventies. We all had our windows down,
and there was fresh air and light and light and light, we four inside
a summer day that allowed us to see snow still up in the Olympics
to our right, thin fields of it gathered there like keepsakes through
these long days; and it was a day that allowed us to see at times the
water to our left, that same blue.

Dad was quiet, looked out his window most of the way, and I can
remember he had a hand to his mouth, in his fingers a Stim-U-Dent,
the mint toothpicks he always had with him.

We headed out of Port Angeles, drove along 101 just as my mom
must have done dozens of times alone, and I remember her talking
behind us, about what a great facility the rehab center would be,
she'd heard even the food was good there, that he'd have his TV from
home set up and be able to watch whatever he wanted, no worries
about fighting with her over which channel.

My dad sat there, a Stim-U-Dent to his mouth, looking out his
window.

Then traffic stopped.

We were still a good 10 miles from Sequim—it was 20 miles
altogether between the two towns—but both our lanes were stopped
completely. No movement at all.

"There's a dangerous spot up a mile or two," my mom said from
behind me, "and I bet there's been another wreck."

I realized then that there were no cars in the oncoming lanes,
both of them empty, and we sat there, unmoving, for twenty minutes.

Mom talked more about the rehab center and yet again about
the Lavender Festival next weekend and how there were farms you
toured and a street fair downtown.

Still Dad said nothing.

Finally, traffic began to move, but only by inches, and after another twenty minutes we came to a state trooper, there in the middle of US 101 in his blue uniform and flat-brimmed hat, flagging each car to detour left off the highway and onto a narrow blacktop headed toward the water.

Up ahead, maybe a mile away, nothing between us on this stretch of road but a trooper waving me off the road, stood a chaos of fire trucks, ambulances, and something destroyed and smoking: a heap of black.

We pulled off, followed the same cars we'd been behind all this while, and found ourselves on a back road, one lane each way and both of them jammed with cars.

We were in pastureland now, broad fields of pale green to either side of us, though the ground just off the blacktop, that shoulder just outside Dad's window, lay thick with wildflowers, reds and purples and oranges.

We were here in the same sunlight as before. Dad had his elbow out in this sunlight, and there, out his window, was the Olympic Range, and that snow, and these flowers, the green pasture.

"This isn't so bad," I said. "This is a great day for a drive."

"It's beautiful out here," my mom said, and Melanie agreed.

Then, after a moment, my dad said, "I want to go up to Butchart Gardens. Victoria. The flowers up there. Gorgeous."

"Yes, we will!" my mom said, maybe too loud. "That's what we'll do. We'll take the ferry out of Port Angeles and make a day of it, maybe stay overnight at a bed and breakfast."

"Yep," Dad said, the toothpick still at his mouth.

I said something more about what a nice drive this was, about how beautiful a day it was, and I meant it. My dad had been inside a hospital room for the last two weeks, yesterday's venture to the end of that street with him in his wheelchair and me pushing it the first time he'd been outside. Now here we were, far away from that hospital and deep in the middle of the country, traffic slow enough to let us take in fully what we had around us.

"I wish we could've stayed for the Lavender Festival," I said.

"Me too," Melanie said.

"You can stop off at one of the farms that'll be on the tour and walk around before you leave, I'm sure," my mom said. "They have shops at the farms and you can walk around." She paused. "But it would have been nice to be here."

Traffic moved.

The rehab center didn't have a room ready for him yet, though his doctor had reserved one earlier in the week, when his leaving the hospital for this element of his healing had become the next real step.

They had his name. They knew who he was. The doctor had reserved a room for him. But they hadn't set one up for him.

Melanie and I stood inside the front entrance, double glass doors behind us, Dad in his wheelchair in front of me. Before us lay a wide pink hallway, a flowery wallpaper border where the walls and ceiling met, a linoleum floor.

It seemed a rest home more than anything else.

To our left was a white Formica counter, in front of it Mom, behind it a woman in pink scrubs who looked at her computer, checked some papers, looked at the computer again. She squinted a smile up at Mom, said, "We've got one he can use for now, then we'll settle him into a regular room."

"I don't understand this at all," my mom said, and I could see she was angry. Her head was tilted to one side, and her eyes wouldn't meet the nurse's, as though my mom were speaking to someone standing just beside the woman. The words were sharp and short, even these few she'd spoken, and she held her hands tight together in front of her on the counter, her purse crooked in her arm.

"Barbara," Dad said then.

"I don't understand this at all," Mom said.

The room the woman led us to was painted the same pink as the hallway, the far wall closed vertical blinds ceiling to floor to hide a sliding glass door. The bed lay to the left, a dresser against the right wall, beside it a mirror, a counter with a chair. To the left of the doorway was the bathroom.

We got Dad into the bed with the help of an orderly in white pants and shirt, then Melanie and I left him and Mom to bring in the suitcase, the box with those framed pictures, and the television. The orderly had given us a cart to roll out there and load up, the TV sitting on top, the rest of his belongings on the shelf beneath. When we came back to the room, Mom was out in the hallway talking to someone else, another, taller woman, this one with glasses but in the same pink scrubs. Now Mom's arms were crossed, her purse still at an elbow, her head tilted still, her words—"Dr. Jones called and arranged for this and ordered his medications to be here and ready, and his menu, and I just don't understand this at all"—still spoken to someone none of us could see.

We went into the room with his gear, and I set the TV on the dresser; Melanie set some photos up on the counter and put the bag beneath it. Then I pulled two more chairs in from the hallway, and Melanie and I sat with Dad, who lay with his eyes closed, quiet. Tired, Melanie and I figured, for what ended up an hour-and-a-half drive from Port Angeles. And for being delivered here, a place he didn't want to go.

Mom was still out in the hallway and talking about how she didn't understand this at all, and then she moved away with the woman to try to call the doctor, to figure out how this could happen.

The room was quiet, the TV not yet on. Just my father, and my wife, and me.

And I heard music, barely audible: a lonesome guitar, a lonely voice.

At first I thought it was music piped into the room through speakers, but even as I scanned the room for them, I thought this wasn't music they'd have played through the place. It was too particular, too old, too *lonesome*.

Life

I stood from my chair, moved past Dad's bed and over to the vertical blinds, still looking for some something that would let me know where this was coming from—were there really speakers? Was there a radio somewhere in here left on?

The music was a little louder now, but still quiet as a thought, and I went to the blinds, twisted the thin plastic wand hanging down.

The sliding glass door looked onto a courtyard maybe 40 feet across, this part of the rehab center built in a square, each room looking out onto it, and the first thing I took in was the sky above it, blue and perfect blue and blue.

I have no word for this blue, for its perfection, its infinity. I do not have the word.

Only a moment—an instant—later I saw, right there out the window, maybe 3 feet away and to my right, an old man sitting in a wheelchair. He had on a flannel shirt, brown corduroy pants. His elbows were on the armrests of the chair, and cradled in one arm was a small boom box. The source of this music.

The music was just a little clearer with the old man this close. It was old cowboy music he was listening to: the thin plaintive tremble of the singer's voice, a tinny slide guitar, somewhere behind it an accordion, a fiddle. I thought it might be Gene Autry, the Gene Autry of old, before "Rudolph" or "Here Comes Santa Claus," playing for an old man sitting alone in a wheelchair in an empty courtyard beneath an impossibly blue sky, listening to him on his boom box.

And now the man, his head down as though he were in prayer but his eyes open, began to move the wheelchair the smallest way with his toe on the ground—he had on an old pair of tennis shoes— so that the chair eased back and forth with the music, maybe an inch at most, back and forth, back and forth.

I cannot make this up.

This is what I thought as I saw this: I cannot make this up. I write novels, I write stories. And this, this: there is no way I could make this up.

As I write this I know I am putting words together that build a moment—ushering one's father to a nursing home only to find him already there in the form of a man alone in a wheelchair, listening to old Gene Autry—as cliché as cliché can possibly be.

But this happened, and my words cannot capture what I want to capture: that sky in its abstract purity above a nursing home on the Olympic Peninsula, the mountains and sea that have accompanied us everywhere but that are now nowhere to be seen, no proof of their existence anywhere; that music and its melancholy solace; the gentle movement of an old man's wheelchair.

Maudlin, sappy, cloyingly sentimental.

And yet this moment of sad wonder happened, while my father lay in his bed behind me, my mother out in a hallway on a mission for the right room, my wife patient in her seat beside his bed.

There is no way to write this.

11

The jet settles now to the tarmac in Tel Aviv. For the last hour or so there has been onboard the predictable bustle that happens as long flights—this one has taken eleven hours—prep for landing: flight attendants have handed out small warm towels, drinks and trash have been gathered, promotional videos of Israel have played, instructions in English and Hebrew and Arabic on how to pass through customs have been broadcast, entry forms have been passed out.

I am in business class, in a bulkhead seat, and as predicted I have not slept. Instead, I have spent much of the night reading Robert Pinsky's translation of *The Inferno*, prepping myself for the seminars on Flannery O'Connor I will be giving the English teachers in Jerusalem. One of the stories I'll be presenting to the class is "The Artificial Nigger," in which a bitter hayseed grandfather takes his insolent grandson on a train ride to the big city of Atlanta, this as a means for the grandfather to show how ugly the city of the grandson's birth truly is. In the story the two quickly become lost, always circling to the left down block after block, drawing deeper and deeper into the bowels of the city, until they arrive finally in an affluent neighborhood where "the big white houses were like partially submerged icebergs."

The parallels between the story and *The Inferno* are undeniable, and so I'd felt obliged to read it again. There were plenty of times during the night when I wanted to stop, to stow the book and forget it; there were plenty of times when I wanted to try to sleep like most everyone in the cabin, at one point during the flight the little spotlight in the ceiling over my seat the only one on.

And I spent much of the night praying, pausing within hell to ask my God to provide the efficiency and care the surgeon who will amputate my father's leg tomorrow morning will need, to comfort my father through all this and to provide the healing that will need to take place, to bless my mother with a calm beyond her understanding through the change this will all mean.

I prayed, because there is no other recourse but to rely upon God, and to surrender to him my fears, and doubt, and feeble faith in him to begin with.

My flight from Denver to Newark yesterday arrived right on time, and I had before me four and a half hours to fill before the 10:50 p.m. flight would leave from the farthest gate on Terminal C. I called Melanie when we landed, asked after any news she might have heard, but there was nothing. Only the time set now for the surgery itself—7:30 tomorrow morning.

I told her I loved her, that I'd call again a time or two before the flight left tonight, then wandered the terminal, briefcase in one hand, small green backpack over a shoulder. I got coffee at Starbucks, then let ego guide me to the Borders bookstore, where

I found one paperback copy of my latest novel, in me a twisted sense of relief for its being there and gloom for how many piles of how many other books surrounded me. I sat in a row of stiff chairs at an empty gate for a while, going through some manuscripts for final consideration for the journal I edit in a far away land called Baton Rouge. I stood before a DVD rental kiosk and considered the prospect, my laptop in my briefcase and who-knew-what to be offered for viewing on the flight, then decided no, I had a book—a long one—to read.

Toward 9:00 I had dinner at the A&W in the food court of Terminal C, sat alone at a wobbly table and ate french fries and a hamburger and drank root beer as if I'd miss American food while I was gone, though I was already looking forward to good falafel and shawarma and hummus. From my table I watched the thickening weal of people headed for the late flight to Tel Aviv at the far reach of the terminal: Hasidic men in their fedoras and bowlers and tendril sideburns, their *tzitzit* fringes peeking now and again from beneath the hems of their black suit coats; their appropriately distanced wives in elegantly drab dresses and their own black hats herding children down the concourse; cancer-thin young people in T-shirts and sunglasses and jeans tight as pantyhose, scarves round their necks, messenger bags strapped across chests; garden-variety tourists in plaid shirts and khakis and tennis shoes: me.

After I finished my root beer I called Melanie again, listened to her, my touchstone, tell me there was nothing further. No word at all, other than that my sister, Leslie, had made it up from Los Angeles, was keeping them company now and would be for the next few days after the surgery.

We agreed—yet one more time—that though this was a terrible thing, it was for the best.

"Try to get some sleep," she told me, "and call me soon as you can when you get there.

"I'll be praying for you," she said, and, "I love you."

Life

The shades on all the windows have been pulled up, and though I am in an aisle seat in the center section, I can see out the window to my right that it is afternoon in Israel: the angle of light gives shadows to the hills far away, and to the baggage truck hauling its containers toward us, and now to the terminal itself out there, the building casting a long flat shadow on the vast concrete field.

It's almost 4:30 here, and I have already done the calculations a hundred times: it's ten hours earlier in a hospital in Port Angeles, Washington, and so right now, right now, it's 8:30 Monday morning. The surgery is happening right now.

The bell dings, and we all stand, pop open the overhead bins, everyone suddenly inside his or her own struggle with the bags up there, and as I am pulling down my backpack stuffed with a change of clothes and toiletries and books for class just in case I lose my checked bag, I hear a woman say over the onboard speakers, "Passenger Bret Lott, please see the gate agent."

For a moment I do not really believe these words. I've never been called out onboard before, never heard my name broadcast like this. Did I really hear my name? Was it my name she said?

But yes. It was.

In the next second it comes to me: last summer, when I came to teach in this same program, I was met at passport control by my driver, a short and heavy man named Shmuel, and because I was here with the State Department he ushered me promptly through a separate passport booth, waved his identification badge at the agent inside, then handed through my passport, and we were done. No waiting at all.

Maybe, I think as I move along the line for the door, my name being called out means that this time Shmuel might meet me at the gate itself, perhaps have a cart for me so that I won't have to walk what last summer had seemed a mile to passport control.

This is what I tell myself.

Ahead of me at the doorway is a tall, officious woman in a uniform of white blouse and blue skirt, directing people to move off the plane as quickly as possible, and doing so in three languages. She waves people through, answers quick questions, waves them through.

But I stop when I get to her, say, "I'm Bret Lott. I'm supposed to talk to the gate agent."

The woman pauses, looks up at me. She lets her eyes meet mine for a moment, then looks at my chest, and with the hand she has used to wave all these people through, she points at me.

"Call your wife," she says.

"Thank you," I say, as though she has given me some kind of small and helpful gift, and I nod, move through.

Immediately—immediately—I think this has to do with one or the other of my two sons; that something bad has happened to Jacob, living and working in Charleston between his sophomore and junior year at the college, or to Zeb, who is living with us in Baton Rouge before he leaves to join the army in October. Something bad has happened to one or the other of them.

This is what I tell myself.

I tell myself, too, that this doesn't have to do with Dad, because the surgery is going on right now. Because it's only an amputation. It's a surgery that will be for the best, despite the fact he will lose his leg.

This is what I tell myself.

I still have to walk the mile to passport control, and so begin the long haul down glass corridor after glass corridor after glass corridor. Toward the end of the trek the glass corridor circles one story above the bustling food court of Ben Gurion Airport so that as we pass we can look through the glass down there at the coffee concession and sandwich restaurant and candy kiosks and vast duty-free store, down there where people sit at tables and mill around, none of them with a phone call to a wife he must make as soon as he can.

This is nothing serious, I tell myself.

This is about Zeb, or Jake. Maybe one or the other has gotten a ticket. Or, maybe, been in an accident. But it's not serious.

Life

Maybe this is just an update on the surgery. This is just to tell me there's a change in the time. But it's not serious.

Then the glass corridors end, and we hustling stream of passengers enter a huge hall, 30 feet wide and perhaps 100 yards long, the ceiling 50 feet above us. The marble floor we walk is angled down, the hall a ramp from the second floor to the first; to my left is an entire wall of glass, afternoon shadows growing longer in the desert air, the brown hills far away out there. And in front of us, at the foot of the ramp, looms a wall of limestone all the way to the ceiling, the wall inset with three mosaic floors, archaeological gems displayed upon the wall like an offering from the country for your simply having entered it.

It is a giant space. It is a humbling space. It is a beautiful and moving space.

And at the bottom of the ramp, in the doorway that leads into passport control, above him this massive wall with its mosaic floors, stands Shmuel, hands on his hips. Then he waves.

I shake his hand when I get to him, tell him I am glad to see him again. He nods, takes my backpack, offers to take my briefcase though I won't let him.

"Miss Jackie is waiting for us," he says in his heavy accent, his voice a kind of rusted metal for the way it rasps. He is short, and heavy, his light blue short-sleeve shirt tucked neatly into black dress pants. He nods over his shoulder, says, "We must go, so give me your passport," the words quick and cluttered in his throat.

"They told me I have to call my wife," I say, but he has already turned, is already through the doorway and walking fast to a booth to our far left, away from the other row of booths with their gathering arrivals. The same booth as last time I was here. He waves his badge to the agent, hands through my passport, but says nothing in response to what I said. The agent glances at me, says something in Hebrew to Shmuel, then nods at me, slips back the passport.

A moment later we are in baggage claim with its shiny rows of oblong carousels, and as if by some strange authority Shmuel has now that I am in his charge, my black rolling duffel is one of the first bags dropped down onto the conveyor belt. I reach for it, but Shmuel, understanding already, snatches it before I can even touch it. He pops out the handle, and we are walking past the customs agents at the far end of the complex, Shmuel nodding to them, me hurrying behind him, and now automatic doors are opening for us, and we are the first people out of customs.

We walk out into yet another massive hall, where there is even more glass and more light, and where too there are hundreds of people gathered to greet all those people still in baggage claim. The crowd stands in a wide circle around us, held in place by a low glass half-wall, the circle 100 feet across, the low wall there so that those exiting customs won't be swarmed by friends and family.

But before me is this huge circle of cleared space which I must walk in a one-man parade behind the efficient Shmuel, who seems to be moving even faster now, people and people and people all looking at me while I walk behind him as fast as I can.

Some of the people hold flowers, and there are balloons out there, too. Some men wear bowlers, and some fedoras, and there are women wearing black hats and drab dresses. There are children, and hip young people, and those in khaki pants and plaid shirts.

All of them know I have a phone call to make to my wife. They all know it, and know too it's nothing serious, most likely a schedule change for my dad's surgery. They all know this, the hundreds of them, the thousands, all standing and waiting, all of them watching.

And now I am nearing the far side of the circle and the pass-through in the glass half wall, where people are knotted even more thickly, waiting and watching, because this is where these people will actually be able to hold and hug and cry and laugh with those arriving, and as Shmuel reaches the crowd, moves past the wall and into those people, I see Jackie Stein standing right there at the crowd's edge, waiting.

Life

Jackie, the cultural programs specialist at the American Center in Jerusalem. She is the one who asked me to come here last year, and again this year. She and her husband, Derek, have already begun looking for leads on an apartment for when Melanie and I will move here in October.

She is a friend.

She is smiling a thin smile. She is wearing a white blouse and brown slacks, her brown-blond hair blunt cut at her shoulders. She is smiling a thin smile.

I make it to her, finally, and these long two days of travel, all the way from Denver to here, are finally complete.

But I have a phone call to make.

"You need to call Melanie," Jackie says. She is from Zimbabwe by way of South Africa, and the accent she brings to my wife's name makes it even more beautiful than it has ever been.

Melanie. The name of my wife. The one I need to call, right now.

"I know," I say, then, "They called my name onboard when we were getting off the plane."

"You can use my phone," she says, and holds out to me a cell phone.

She isn't smiling now. Shmuel stands a few feet behind her, the rolling duffel leaned into him, the handle in his hand, my backpack in his other. He is looking at me as well, and he isn't smiling, either. And there are all these people here. All these people.

I say, "Where's the car? Let's go get in the car first, and then I'll call. I probably couldn't hear anything in here anyways."

I cannot make this up.

Jackie's eyes are on mine a moment, her lips pinch a moment just as quick, and she says, "Are you sure you don't want to call her?"

"It'll be better if we're in the car," I say, and look past her to Shmuel, nod at him. "Let's go out to the car," I say and smile at him. He gives a mechanical smile, a twitch at the corners of his mouth. But he is looking at Jackie. Not me.

I look at Jackie, who is trying at a smile.

Then she quickly turns to Shmuel, nods, says to him, "Let's go." She turns back to me, slips the phone into the purse hanging from her shoulder. She nods, and we are headed for the glass doors out of here.

There is a case to be made for my not wanting to make a phone call there in the greeting hall at Ben Gurion Airport. It is a case that would involve the crowd around us, all those people and all that noise. It is a case that might also include my knowing this was nothing serious, that there had simply been a change in the schedule for my father's surgery, or that one of my sons had gotten a ticket.

But this case, were I to make it here as I made it to myself then, would be only a coward's plea. I was a coward, seeking only one last moment to keep from receiving what I had already been given.

I was trying to stop from stepping through to this world, where what had not yet happened was now in the past.

And I am summoning the words to begin. I am summoning them now, on the morning of October 16, 2009, a morning at which it has taken me three years and ninety-eight days to arrive, when I can write with words I can neither trust nor deny:

"I'm so sorry to tell you this, but your father died last night."

This is Melanie's voice on Jackie's cell phone. We are driving away from the airport, Shmuel beside me and behind the wheel, Jackie in the seat behind.

I am the one who insisted we drive away from the airport before I made the call. I am the one who insisted we head for Jerusalem, and the hotel, because this wouldn't be anything serious, this phone call.

The exitway from the airport is a wide black swath in this desert. Out my window are manicured rows of orange trees, dark and waxy green. Out Shmuel's window is a parking area, shrubs, and far away the Judean hills.

"Oh," I say. I say, "Oh. Okay."

Melanie is quiet for a few seconds, then says, "It was a surprise. It happened last night, when Leslie was there. About nine o'clock. Your mom had gone home for a little while to take a shower."

"Oh," I say. "Okay."

I'd known this was what the phone call would be about all along.

If I had believed it was merely a change in a surgery schedule, I would have made the call right then, unafraid of others around me. And if I had believed it was about one of my children, I would have run from the Jetway to that cell phone in Jackie Stein's hand.

I'd known.

12

Of the thirteen books I have published, eleven of them came out while he was alive. Of those eleven, I do not believe my father read more than three.

I do not say this as an indictment of him. I do not write this as an accusation made in any sort of resentment or see this as a sin against me. Rather, it is simply a fact that he didn't read much, and I can only recall ever hearing from him about three of those books.

The first was my first book, the novel *The Man Who Owned Vermont*, published in 1987. It is about an RC salesman whose job, in its own way, seems to offer the narrator a kind of salvation. But it is an empty salvation, because what genuinely matters—his wife, and their love for each other—is fast on its way out of his life.

After he read it, my father told me, "You think working for RC was a waste." I'd tried to explain to him that this wasn't the case at all, that what he'd read was a novel, a made-up story, and that just because the narrator thrives on being a salesman for RC yet doesn't love his job doesn't mean I felt that way.

He'd missed the point of the book, I'd wanted to tell him, but didn't. It wasn't about RC but about love.

The next book I know he read was my fourth one, the novel *Jewel*, published in 1991. It is a book based on his own family, the narrator inspired by my dad's mother and those six children she bore, the last of which, his youngest sister, was a Down syndrome baby. It is a long book, and traces the lives of those children and the life of Jewel's marriage to her husband, Leston; it traces as well the parallel and intersecting and, finally, deeply divergent lives of the narrator and a friend named Cathedral.

My father thought this was a terrific book, told me I'd gotten the family and its saga exactly right, though when I'd written it I'd lived in an imaginary place called Mississippi, in a time long before I'd been born. I'd imagined it all.

The only other book I know him to have read was *Fathers, Sons, and Brothers*, that book in which I tried to hold still for a moment those moments we were all of us living inside. He'd enjoyed it, he told me, and appreciated especially seeing the family pictures the publisher had thought to include in the text.

Beyond those small conversations—no more than comments, actually—on those three books, I cannot recall much of anything else from him, and nothing on any of the other books. Of course when *Jewel* became an Oprah pick, the book a best seller within the day it was announced, things changed: I was suddenly Famous. By this time—February of 1999—he was a food broker at a firm in Tustin, and when people in his office began to bring copies of the book to him to have me sign them, and when a movie was gearing up to be made, and when there were articles in *People* and a few weeks on the best-seller lists and me, his son, on *Oprah*, he wrote me a letter.

He'd never written me one before.

This was in April of that year, me in town for the *Los Angeles Times* Festival of the Book at UCLA, where I would be speaking with two other Oprah authors on what it all was like. Zeb would soon be turning sixteen, and for his birthday Melanie and I decided he could come along with me, the two of us put up by the publisher at the Century Wilshire Hotel. We got in Friday afternoon and saw *The Matrix* at the Westwood Village, then ate Thai at a restaurant a couple doors down before spending Saturday at the Festival. Sunday morning we drove a rental car down to Irvine to visit Mom and Dad for a couple of days. They'd sold the house in Huntington Beach, downsized into a condominium complex with a narrow yard full of ivy and a yard crew to do what little work there was to maintain it.

Monday morning, Zeb still asleep and me with Mom and coffee at their dining room table, my dad asked me if I'd come down to his office later on, told me there were people he worked with who wanted to meet me, maybe sign some more books for them. He was already dressed and ready to go, had on his brown blazer and black pants and blue tie. He had some work to get to, and I could drive over later on.

Of course I said yes. Zeb would be spending most of the day surfing with my old housemate from college days, Dave Royster, though Zeb's surfing in South Carolina would have prepared him, we all knew, for nothing he would encounter at the pier at Huntington. I had the time. Sure, I'd come by.

Later that morning, I pulled into the parking lot of his brokerage firm there in Tustin, the building like a million others in Southern California: stucco, glass, this parking lot out front. I went inside, gave my name to the receptionist, who was nodding and smiling before I'd said a thing, and had me sign a book before my dad made it out to meet me. Then he introduced me around to those people for whom I'd already signed books, had me sign a few more, and I could see in the way he introduced me—his laugh, his voice broad and full, him smiling and smiling—that he was proud of me.

Lastly, he introduced me to his boss, a man with short red hair who looked twenty years younger than my dad. He had on a white dress shirt and red tie and black pants, and no jacket. He looked me in the eye, smiled, congratulated me and thanked me for having signed a book for him a couple weeks ago.

I smiled and nodded, smiled and nodded. But what I was thinking about was how much younger this man was than my dad, and that this man who was my dad's boss wasn't wearing a jacket, while here stood my dad in a brown herringbone tweed blazer, a bold blue tie. And now I saw that the three or four other men I'd been introduced to didn't have jackets on either, and now it came to me that all of them—eight or nine people—gathered here in the reception area to see Bill's son, the Famous Writer, were all younger than him. Every one.

But I only smiled and nodded, because there was nothing else to do save tuck away this detail for here, now, as I write it.

We walked out to the parking lot, and as I climbed into my rental, he pulled from the inside breast pocket of that brown blazer a piece of yellow lined paper, torn from a tablet and folded in thirds.

He handed it to me, sitting there with the car door open. He said, "This is a letter for you. You can read it later on. But I just wanted you to know I'm proud of you."

I looked up at him. He was squinting for the sun out here. But I could see he was smiling, too.

I said, "Thank you." I said, "I appreciate that."

"See you tonight," he said, and tapped the roof of the car, then turned and headed back inside.

I read it there in the parking lot. It was written in black ink, the messy scrawl his handwriting always was. But I could read it.

In it he told me he was proud of me, that he was happy people could read this story of his mother and know what a good person she was, what a difficult life she'd had. He was proud of me.

I would like in this moment to quote that letter. But I cannot, because I do not know where it is.

I have spent just now two hours going through the black plastic

storage bins my papers are kept in out in the garage, seeking out
that piece of lined yellow paper. There are twenty-three bins, and
while going through them I found plenty of things I hadn't seen
in years, remembered events I'd attended and people I'd known
and things I'd written that I'd forgotten for the cloud of life always
with me.

I prayed I would find the letter, because I wanted to hold it and
share what he said in these too-many pages of another essay about
the death of a father. I wanted to get his written words in here, so
that I could hear him again, but also so that I might seem a better
son than I have turned out to be.

Because one of the things I know about fatherhood and sonship
and the river that runs between the two is that not often enough
do sons receive from their fathers words like the ones he wrote me.

Instead, I have cradled like icons those two letters and the postcard from Raymond Carver, a man I never knew and who didn't
know me, and misplaced the one I received from my father.

The only other time—and the last—I heard from my father
about something I'd written was in July 2003, when I was asked
back to the Port Townsend Writers' Conference to teach at its thirti-
eth anniversary. By this time he'd quit the brokerage firm to retire,
and because two of their four children lived in the Seattle area—Tim
and Bridget in Sumner, Brad and Joan in Sequim—and because
they'd been to Sequim a few times over the years and enjoyed it, and
because living in Southern California cost so very much, he and my
mother had moved to Sequim in February of that year.

Here my parents lived in a duplex apartment a block behind a
strip mall with a QFC grocery store, a Swain's Hardware, and that
frozen yogurt place I'd taken Brad and Joan and my nieces to when
I'd first come to this place. Here my parents found a community
where, because Sequim is a retirement town, most everyone was
their own age. Here they found a church they both seemed to enjoy,

and the routine of Sunday brunch afterward with a small gang of friends they were coming to know.

And because now there were so many of my family already in this one place, Mom decided we should all get together in Sequim while I was teaching at the conference, and that we would have a family portrait done, and we could rent rooms at a hotel on Sequim Bay and make a reunion out of it all.

Zeb and Jake were working summer jobs, Zeb between his sophomore and junior year in college, Jake about to be a high school senior, and arrangements had to be made for them to take off work a few days each, fly them from Charleston to Seattle and back. Leslie and her husband John's kids were a little younger—Daniel was fifteen, Marcus twelve, Isabel eight, and Chloe only a few months old—and so were a bit more flexible, but a brood all the same. Alyson was living in Seattle by then, Rachel still at home with Brad and Joan. It would be difficult to get us all there. But we could do it.

Though I'd been assigned the same barracks rooms at Fort Worden as last time, we stayed at the hotel, me driving back and forth between Sequim and Port Townsend the few days we were all there together. We barbequed at Brad and Joan's, went for breakfast at Gwennie's Restaurant on the main drag, hung out in the rooms on Sequim Bay, and played board games. One afternoon all eighteen of us stood in a gazebo at a park, each family unit wearing a different color shirt—ours were red—while a photographer took a hundred shots.

And one evening during this all, I gave a reading at the conference.

I've given dozens and dozens of readings in my life, but the only family members ever present were Melanie and, once, my brother Brad, who came to the reading I'd given at this same conference back in 1997, when he and his family were still living in that trailer. Not even my two sons had seen me read.

Now all of them were here, in Wheeler Theater at Fort Worden.

Life

Seventeen of them, taking up a large block of the room toward the back—the place seated around 250 altogether—just in case baby Chloe began to fuss and Leslie needed to get out quickly.

I do not remember being more nervous about a reading before this. There was and remains something strangely and comfortably anonymous about reading to crowds of people you don't know, something that allows me to pass through the fear that speaking in front of people can engender. Of course I get nervous, fearing perhaps I will skip a page, or mispronounce a word, or swallow in a bad place or cough. Of course I get nervous.

But this was different. Though the theater was full, there were people, that whole bank of rows back there, who knew me. They were family.

I read an essay called "Toward Humility." It is, at least for me, an odd essay, written in second person and moving backward in time, section by section, to reveal the story of what it is like to have had a book one has written chosen by an international celebrity for her book club. It begins after she has chosen it and the second person—you—is flying in a private jet to a book signing; it ends before the book has been chosen, when you are a little-known writer making a fool of yourself at your younger son's soccer game because a new book you are writing is failing miserably. It is about the self-involved, self-inflicted misery of working on something you know isn't going to work, and about the gift the writing of other books can be—specifically that one you wrote about a woman and her family and her Down syndrome daughter, the book that will, unbeknownst to you, be picked in a month to become a best seller.

"There are more important things than a book," the you of the essay says near the end, when at the soccer game you have successfully, if unintentionally, alienated your older son sitting on the sidelines, the younger son out on the field, and your wife, who loves you but wordlessly lets you know what a fool you are. All because of your preoccupation with "a stupid book."

It is about, finally, my forgetting to get out of the way.

There had been the usual hubbub once the reading was over, students in the conference coming up and thanking me, my signing a few books, all that. My eye, though, was on the back of the theater, where I could see my family sort of milling about, waiting. Dad stood there with his hands in his pockets, Mom talking to Melanie, who was nodding. My sister, Chloe on her hip, managed a wave to me, and I nodded. My boys were already heading out the door with Marcus and Daniel and Alyson and Rachel, while my brother Tim put a fist to the side of his eye and twisted it, made like he was crying, his mouth in a big sad frown: yanking my chain.

I finally made it back to them, and we all went outside, climbed in our cars, and drove the quarter mile or so over to my rooms in the barracks. The plan was for us all to just sit and relax for a while before heading back to Sequim, to let people see what these barracks were like, to just talk.

By this time in my dad's life his diabetes had begun its work in earnest: he couldn't walk very well, his eyesight failing. He'd also grown cranky, though using this word is a pleasant way to say he'd become more and more contentious, more churlish over the last ten years. We all assigned this to the fact he'd retired, had no job to report to every day; he also had no yard work to do anymore, not since they'd moved out to Irvine and that condo with the ivy and a yard crew. But we also knew his gruffness was due in a large way to the diabetes. Since moving to Sequim earlier that year his daily life had been whittled down to a visit to the QFC for coffee, a short walk to the small park at the end of their street, and watching TV in the living room of their duplex. He was still driving, not that he had anywhere to go but because, we all knew, were he to stop driving he would become even worse, grow even more difficult.

His life, it is easy to see as I write this, was in decline. He would live for only three more years.

And on this night his contentiousness, his churlishness, made itself plain once we were all in the front room of the barracks, sitting or perched upon the mismatched furniture spread through the room: a wicker armchair, a blocky '70s sofa with arms as high as its back, a loveseat, spindly chairs from the dining room table and equally spindly side tables upon which sat homely lamps with dented shades. The kids were all outside messing around in the growing dark; only Chloe was with us, still on Leslie's hip.

We had a fight.

Dad, sitting in an overstuffed chair with lace doilies on the arms to hide the worn fabric, claimed loudly that I hated being a writer, but that that was my job and I better get used to it and that I'd better like it because that was my work.

Leslie argued that the essay hadn't been about that at all. It had been about family, and how much I loved my boys and Melanie.

Tim said he thought it was a good story, and that he thought the way I looked at writing was the right way, because there were more important things in your life than work.

Brad agreed.

The spouses kept quiet, Melanie and Bridget and John and Joan all with sense enough to stay out of the fray.

My mother agreed with Tim and Leslie and Brad and said that there was no reason my dad should be like this on the night when his son had given a reading in a beautiful theater with all those people who seemed to really like it, and wasn't that part about signing a book to a dog for that crazy old lady funny?

My dad, his voice rising, hands flat on those doilies, said I hated my job, and that work was good, and if I hated writing so much I ought to quit.

I sat in one of the spindly chairs, watching and listening and being overwhelmed, because I'd never seen my dad get this worked up about something I'd written and had never heard my sister and brothers engage like this over the same words they'd all taken in. Early on I made a stab to defend what I'd done and remember saying, "I was trying to put in perspective what's important." But as soon as I'd heard my own words out of me, I realized the feebleness of any defense and felt in the same moment thankful for my family, all doing their best to tell my dad he was wrong.

The evening broke up not long after, when we all seemed to calm down and talk turned, my mom leading the way, to that scene in the essay about signing a book for a dog, and then the one about flying in the private jet with Jacob, and about how Melanie really did pick up her lawn chair there on the sidelines of the soccer game and without a word move 50 feet away from me hollering on at Jacob about how he was playing, when it was a stupid book I was really mad about, and then we gathered the kids, and drove on back to Sequim.

I did not hold my dad's argument against him. More than anything, his missing the point of the essay, or at least what I had hoped was the point, saddened me, and I said as much to Melanie as we were climbing into bed that night.

"His whole life was working," she said, stating square and true, as I have come to count on her doing, what the deep matter was. "He doesn't work anymore and wishes he did. Of course he'd get angry when you said work wasn't the most important thing in your life. For him, it still is."

Then the next morning, as if making amends somehow for what my dad had said, my mom talked him into going with Melanie and me on an excursion over to Port Angeles. Melanie and I drove from the hotel to their duplex intending just to stop in on our way, the boys staying to hang out with Daniel and Marcus and everyone else. But Mom had the big idea to accompany us on this jaunt we were making, and Dad didn't so much agree as simply stand and move slowly for the door and then on out to the driveway and our car and climb into the front passenger seat.

We stopped first at the Starbucks at the Safeway out past Gwennie's—a real treat after having had QFC's coffee the last couple of days—and then drove the 20 miles of dips and curves and level ground of US 101, the Olympic Range always to our left, the water to our right, and then through congested, industrial, beat-up Port Angeles.

"We don't make it over here very much," my mom said from the seat behind me, Melanie behind Dad, and then when we turned off 101 at the far end of town and into what seemed a residential area, my dad said, "You're sure you know where you're going?"

"Why do you like this writer so much?" my mom asked for the tenth time, and my dad said once again, "I never heard of him."

A moment later, at the end of a row of trees on our right, we pulled onto a narrow driveway, and so into Ocean View Cemetery.

It was an overcast day this time, not at all the clear blue of the first time I'd been here with Brad. But there was still this view: the Strait of Juan de Fuca, the edge of Canada across it, above it all a huge and brooding gray sky.

"Oh my," my mom said from behind me. "This is beautiful."

I eased the car along the gravel lane, my eye already on the black granite bench up ahead on my left, that metal arch in front of it, and the flowers there.

This was Melanie's first time here, too. "This really is beautiful," she said, and I felt her touch my shoulder.

Dad said nothing.

I edged off the lane into the grass to allow through anyone else who might show up while we were here, then turned off the engine, opened my door. Melanie already had her door open, too, and came around the back of the car, smiling at me standing there, waiting with my hand out to her. She took it, and we started across the grass toward the grave. She'd been with me when I first met Raymond Carver, had been the one to nudge me, more than twenty years before, the last few feet toward him in that crowded room at UNH.

There were just as many flowers clustered up at that arch as when I'd been here six years before, as though he had died only a little while ago. But before we made it the few yards to that bench and its view, I looked behind me to see how my mom and dad were doing.

They both stood at the car, their doors still open, my dad on the far side, my mom on this side. But they weren't looking over here, where Melanie and I were headed.

They were both looking out at the water, and this view.

Then my mother turned to us. "Bury me here," she said, her words certain and strong. She wasn't smiling. She meant it.

"Me too," my dad said a moment later, his two small words just as strong, just as certain. But he hadn't turned to us, only stood leaning against his open car door, looking at the view.

They bought plots there less than a month later.

13

I watched the old man in the wheelchair under the blue sky outside my dad's room for only a minute or so. I was afraid he might glance up at me and see me staring at him from inside, while still he toed the chair back and forth with the music, Gene Autry and that fiddle and accordion and guitar his only company in the world.

Then I twisted the thin plastic wand, closed the vertical blinds back up.

My mother returned to the room, let us know her mission to get Dad the right room here at the rehab center and the medications ordered and his menu set had yielded nothing. Today was the day before the Fourth of July, a Monday, and though their doctor was out of town for the weekend he would be in tomorrow; the taller woman with glasses and those pink scrubs—the shift supervisor—could only verify that Dad was supposed to be here, but beyond that there had come no instructions from anyone. The supervisor had called the hospital, taken down the menu he'd had, but because none of the medications he was on were life-saving, the woman had reasoned, there were no immediate worries: he was recovering, hence he'd been sent here. He'd be fine the rest of the day and through the night, and the doctor would be here first thing tomorrow morning to see him.

These things made sense, though there was still in my mom and in Melanie and in me a feeling Dad had fallen through a crack before we'd ever even arrived.

Eventually Gene Autry, as quiet as he had been all along, faded away, and I went to the window again, with a finger pushed back a single blind to see the man was gone.

And Dad, as well as he had seemed the day before when I'd pushed him to the cafeteria, then outside to look at the view and to feel the wind and sun, smell the ocean, seemed suddenly even quieter than before. He spoke now and again, said he needed to go to the bathroom, a request the orderly helped him with while I stood and held the door; he asked for some water with ice to drink. When he spoke it was with a full voice, too, no feebleness or waning energy. But between these requests, and as the day led on to night, he lay quiet in bed, his eyes closed all the while.

Melanie and I decided during the course of the afternoon that Mom, in and out of the room again and again in her efforts to get whatever the right room meant—this one seemed to me as right a room as one might get in this facility—needed a night away from this watch she had been keeping for more than two weeks now, and so when she returned yet one more time with no news other than how disappointed she was in all parties involved, we informed her that Melanie was taking her to get a bite to eat and then out to a movie. Did she want to go see *The Devil Wears Prada*?

She stood there in the room and wrung her hands over this decision. We'd never turned on any lights, the early evening glow from behind the blinds and the indifferent fluorescent pall from the hallway outside the only light in here.

"You're going," Melanie said, and in this way the matter was solved.

Dad seemed to sleep. The room was quiet, the hallway outside quiet as well. Now and again a nurse leaned in, checked to see if he was all right. Melanie and Mom promised to bring me something back for dinner—they wouldn't be too late, the movie starting at 7:00—and once the glow from outside had disappeared entirely, I turned on the TV, there on top of the dresser, and put the volume as low as I could and still make out sound.

I didn't even change channels. I only wanted the TV to play, though on its bright and colorful screen was an absolutely awful program, a cheap reality show that was a cross between *The Amazing Race* and the movie *National Treasure*. As far as I could tell, teams of contestants were going around the world and finding puzzle pieces and had to scheme a way to get a treasure somewhere. It was stupid, insipid, asinine, awful.

I watched it.

I sat in a room with my father and still felt the lingering sadness of an old man in a wheelchair, and of a slow drive through pastures and wildflowers, and a view of the sea and the feel of cold wind at the end of a street. I wanted the TV to keep me company somehow, but to ask of me nothing. I didn't want to read, because that would make me truly leave the room and so my father; for this same reason I didn't want to try to find something good to watch on TV, or even to step outside the room for a walk down the hall and back.

And as I write this, I realize the words I am searching for, the description just beyond my reach until this moment, is this: I was keeping vigil.

My father was dying, I knew deeply, intrinsically, though I cannot say that I believed this while I was sitting with him, because he was recovering, he would begin physical therapy at this rehab center later this week, he was out of the hospital in Port Angeles and back here in Sequim.

But I knew. It was in this sudden quiet that had come over him since we'd gotten here, and the full voice with which he'd said he needed to go to the bathroom, and that same odd strength with which he called for a sip of ice water. His coming death was here in the darkness of this room, too, though I could abolish it with a quick touch to a switch plate; and his coming death was in the mountains outside still holding snow in July, in that blue sea not far from here, and in my own heart as I sat alone with him and watched drivel—people were walking down a dark stone corridor now, looking for something—on a TV brought from his own house and settled here for as long as he would stay.

"Please turn that down," he said from nowhere, and I jumped at his words, so clear and strong, so calm and certain.

I turned to him, saw him in the bed, the light off the TV playing vaguely across his face and the blanket tucked under his chin, only his head visible. His eyes were closed. He seemed asleep.

"I'm sorry," I said, and quickly mashed the volume button on the remote until there was no sound at all. I said, "Do you need any ice water or anything?"

"No," he said. That was it.

As though I'd made an important but empty pact with it, I watched the muted program until its finish, then turned off the TV altogether. I sat in darkness now, and watched him lying there. On occasion he took in a single deep, heavy breath, then let it out, as though he were remembering it was time to breathe. And it was during this time that I prayed for him: for the healing of the sores on his legs, for the rehabilitation of his legs, for the people who worked here who would be helping him to walk again, and for his doctor. I prayed, because there was no other recourse but to rely upon God and to surrender to him my fears, and doubt, and feeble faith in him to begin with. I prayed, because I knew but could not believe he was dying.

Later, Melanie and Mom came in. Melanie had hold of a plastic bag with a Styrofoam tray in it: something I was to eat. My mom seemed delighted to have gone to the movies, carried on in a loud whisper about how good Meryl Streep was and that young girl who played her assistant and what a treat it was to go to the movies. Then she turned and headed to the nurses' station to see what more she could find out about the right room.

We finally left around 10:30, nothing further to do for Dad but be present in his room while he tried to sleep. My mom stood by his bed and touched at the blanket here and there, as though it weren't already still neatly tucked in beneath his chin. She told him she loved him, that we'd all be back in the morning, and not to worry. My dad said nothing, only took in another deep breath, and then we left.

14

"I'm sorry," I say to Jackie, and hand her back the phone. "I'm sorry. I should have called her in the airport."

"Don't apologize," she says. "Don't. I understand. I do. We just need to see about getting you a seat on the next flight back."

But because I did not call Melanie from inside the airport, me seeking to hide within my cowardice from what I knew I would discover once I made the call, Shmuel is already driving the wide black swath of the exit-way from Ben Gurion airport, and out to the freeway.

But there's a lane that peels off on the left that goes back to the airport, and Shmuel follows it, out his window still the parking area, shrubs, the Judean hills far away, still out my window the manicured rows of dark and waxy orange trees. We go through the security post, armed soldiers peering inside the car as Shmuel hands our passports out his window. The soldier in charge, a young woman who wears aviator sunglasses, says nothing, only looks at the documents the briefest moment, hands them back in. A minute later we pull in precisely where we started: the covered strip of reserved parking spots outside the greeting hall.

We go inside, Shmuel leading us through the hall, people still clustered and waiting for family and friends to emerge from customs, then back past the bank of ticket agents to the inner workings of the airlines themselves, where we find the customer service office for the airline.

Behind the counter is the same woman who dispatched me from the door of the airplane, tall and officious in her white blouse and blue skirt.

With both Jackie's and Shmuel's assistance, we work through getting me a seat on the next available flight out—tomorrow morning at 11:00—and it seems there is some sort of hidden cachet given me suddenly, that in the concerned way the agent looks up from the monitor and keyboard in front of her to meet my eyes with a question and then another and another, that something has happened, that there is some status to what we are doing, some importance and deeper meaning.

I am puzzled a moment, wondering why this transaction is being handled as simply and promptly and cleanly as it is. This woman in her white blouse and blue skirt is no longer officious, no longer the nearly curt gate agent dispatching in three languages all questions thrown at her.

Instead, she is courteous, and gracious, and humble.

I am puzzled. But only for a moment, and I see in this deferential treatment, in the nod of her head as she prints out the boarding pass for the flight from here to Newark, and then the pass for the connection to Seattle—it will be another very long day of travel tomorrow—and then in the sad smile she gives me when she hands them to me, and her quick words "I'm sorry for your loss"—I see in all this that I have been ushered somewhere else.

I am in a different place. I am suddenly and irrevocably in the future, I now understand. I am standing where what hadn't yet happened was now in the past.

"Thank you," I say to her, and nod, and smile. As though any of this were a gift.

Jackie says from the back seat, "Melanie told me when she called me. So I knew when we were in the airport what had happened. I wanted so badly to insist you make the call. But I simply couldn't make you. I couldn't very well come out and tell you why." Her voice is sad, and careful, and in the same moment has a kind of cheerful edge to it: she hasn't been in this situation before and is doing her best.

I am looking out on the countryside, the hills off to our left and growing closer, the flat plain to the right that leads away to the Mediterranean. In the distance out my window, a couple miles away and like some giant mechanical ghost through the thin haze of late afternoon air, is what looks like an electrical plant.

"You're right," I say. "I should have called her then. I just thought it would be better to come outside and call where it was quieter." I turn and look back at her, shake my head. "The thing is that he was just going in for surgery. He wasn't supposed to die. I thought it was going to be something about his surgery. Or maybe about Zeb or Jake. Something small."

I say this, about the surprise of it, and that I believed it was something else, because I am still a coward. And I am just now in this new world.

We talk more—Jackie about the program and how I will be missed but that she thinks it can get along this year without me, that they'll figure a way through this; me about the surprise of what has happened, about how even though he lives outside Seattle and we live in Baton Rouge, I just saw him six days ago, on the Fourth of July at the end of the vacation Melanie and I had taken out west; Jackie about the apartment she and Derek haven't yet found for us, and how remarkable a thing it is that we will be living here beginning in October.

Shmuel, quiet, drives the wide freeway at a speed faster than safe, but I don't care. We are going to Jerusalem, and despite the fact Jackie and I are exchanging words about different subjects, despite the way we are conversing about life ahead and what we will do to accommodate ourselves to those plans—to make way for the life that hasn't yet happened but which we believe will come to pass—I have news in me, right here, right now, that I do not know what to do with. Between now and when Shmuel will pick me up tomorrow morning at 8:00, there are fourteen hours I will have to spend, and I am beginning them, now.

"Derek's going to meet us at Mishkenot," Jackie says. "We'll get you checked in, let you settle in a little bit, and then, of course, doing anything is up to you. But we thought you'd want to get something to eat. We thought perhaps we could walk over to German Colony and have dinner, and if you wanted to, you could say hello to Andrea and ML. They're already checked in, and both want to say hello to you. And then you can go back to your room and get some sleep." She pauses. "Provided any of this is what you want to do. It's all up to you."

As soon as she's said the word *Mishkenot*, I am there at the long and low limestone guest house and cultural center—Mishkenot Sha'ananim—that looks out across the rocky Hinnom Valley to the walls of the old city only a couple hundred yards away. I stayed there last year when I taught with the program, and know how quiet a place it is, austere for that limestone, the spare furnishings, the cool tile floors. There are maybe two dozen guest rooms in all, a sitting room and bedroom for each, and each with a double door off that sitting room onto a shared portico that runs the entire length of the flat-roofed building. Two chairs and an end table sit on the portico outside each room so that guests can relax and look out on the valley, and the old city.

Which is where, now that she has reminded me, I am already. I am already sitting outside on the portico, and looking at the walls of Jerusalem.

"That's good," I say. "Let's get some dinner. And I want to meet ML, and see Andrea."

Andrea: the State Department English teaching officer, with whom I taught last summer; ML: the poet I haven't yet met except through e-mails leading up to this event. My co-teachers for what was to have been the next two weeks.

Suddenly, though they have been in sight since pulling out of the airport, here beside us are the hills, orange now for the sun low in the sky behind us, and the freeway narrows as it peels to the left and into a valley, and we begin our ascent to Jerusalem.

We pass the rusted carcasses of military vehicles, left in the valley since 1948 as remembrances of the war. The hills grow steeper and steeper, all terraced with olive trees, the sun hidden now behind us, and then finally, finally, the freeway now hugging the upper edges of the cliffs in the valley, I can see ahead of us the huge cemetery at the edge of Jerusalem proper, flat stones that carpet the mountainside, and then we are in the snarled knot of city traffic.

We snake our way through modern buildings and parks, high-rise condos and townhouses, up and up, the streets filled with people dressed the same as those I'd seen in the airport last night in Newark—Hassidim and tourists and the terminally hip alike—a city alive with itself at dusk of a July evening, and then we are through one clogged intersection and another, the street we are on cresting and then falling down the other side.

We turn left onto a small curl of a street lined with walls of limestone leading farther down this hill, and now there is an iron gate before us, and Shmuel stops the car: security for Mishkenot Sha'ananim.

Shmuel says nothing, only waits, and then the gate slowly opens. He pulls the car through, eases around the curve to the turn-around out front of the glass wall entry to the cultural center and guest house.

Shmuel quickly climbs out, already has the trunk open and my black rolling duffel and green backpack in hand before I can even get to the rear of the car. We follow him through the glass doors into a wide and cool reception area, limestone walls and floors, and Jackie takes over at the front desk to check me in.

"Eight o'clock tomorrow morning," Shmuel says from behind me, his voice that same rusted metal, and I turn to him. "I see you then," he says, and smiles, nods once. Then, "I am sorry."

The smile is gone, and he dips his chin a little, his eyebrows together. He nods once more.

"Thank you," I say, and he turns, heads away toward those glass doors.

I walk along the open-air hall toward my room, Jackie waiting up at the desk. "Just settle into your room and take your time," she said before I left her there. "Derek will be here in a moment, and when you're ready we can go get a bite to eat."

And so I left, went to the elevator and took it down the one floor to the atrium-like breezeway, started for my room.

Photographs line the wall to my right, framed eight-by-ten glossies every few feet, of people who have stayed here: Pablo Casals, Saul Bellow, Grace Paley, Isaac Stern, the Dalai Lama, and more. Mishkenot Sha'ananim is a state-run private facility, the people who stay here all screened and vouched for. When I was here last year and saw these same pictures I marveled at them, and at me, here at this same center, a guest here too. But as I look at them this time, me with my backpack over one shoulder, briefcase in hand, the rolling duffel behind me making a low plastic rumble as it rolls across the limestone floor, I feel nothing.

This nonfeeling isn't because I am grieving. No. Not grief.

But I do not yet know what it is.

I am a person walking down the limestone hallway of this guest house, a piece of news residing in me I do not know how to hold, how to carry, where to put, or how even to consider.

All I can do is arrive at my door, insert the key and turn the knob, enter the cool sitting room with its sofa and coffee table and desk, a copy of this day's *Jerusalem Post* centered on it, then move into the bedroom and set my duffel and backpack and briefcase on the bed. All of which I do.

Because I am here.

But when I come out of the bedroom and back into the sitting room, I let myself look at them: two double doors leading off the rear of the room.

I know what they open onto. I know what you can see from just beyond them. I know there are two chairs and an end table out on the portico on the other side of these two doors, where one can sit and look at the walls of the old city. Of Jerusalem.

Just outside those double doors is a place to rest, and to be alone.

But not yet.

Instead, I sit down at the desk in the sitting room, and call Melanie, and we talk.

15

The last time I saw my father alive was when I said good-bye to him the morning of the Fourth of July, 2006. A Tuesday.

Melanie, Mom, and I ate breakfast—cereal, coffee, English muffins—there in Mom and Dad's duplex. Melanie and I had already packed our bags, had loaded them into the rental car, our vacation winding down. Once we'd say good-bye to Dad that morning, we'd drive on over to Sumner, outside Tacoma, where we'd spend the rest of the day at Tim and Bridget's house, then fly out of Seattle to Baton Rouge early tomorrow.

And so, given the writer's conference in Salt Lake City I'd taught the week before we'd headed out on this western tour, and all the travel and teaching and talking about writing writing writing I had in front of me, this road trip had served well as a respite from the world. We'd visited with Melanie's aunt and uncle at Lake Tahoe, hiked to the top of Vernal and Nevada Falls in Yosemite, and spent all that time driving, the two of us together.

Life

But it had finished this way, with our pulling in at the hospital in Port Angeles two days ago, and then with our taking him from the hospital back here to Sequim and the center yesterday.

"Please turn that down," my father had said from beside me in the dark of his room last night, the blanket tucked to his chin, while I'd sat there watching crappy television.

I'd jumped at his words, so clear and strong, so calm and certain.

We rinsed our dishes, and listened one more time to Mom go on about how sorry she was we would be missing the Lavender Festival this weekend, and how there were tours of the lavender farms you could take this weekend if only we were here, and the street fair they had and the parade too, and how sorry she was we'd miss the whole thing.

But we could go see if one of the farms would let us walk around because they were all getting ready for this weekend anyway. The best one was Jardin du Soleil, we passed right by it on our way to the Three Crabs the other night, remember? So you know right where it is. You really should go over there before you head over to Tim and Bridget's, you really should.

So we agreed, Melanie and I, to go visit the place on our way out of town, though it wasn't really on our way. We would visit a lavender farm.

We followed Mom then to the rehab center. The sky had turned overcast, all that blue gone, and we drove past the strip mall with the QFC, Swain's Hardware, that frozen yogurt place. Then across the overpass for 101, the Olympic Range now out our windshield, and into the parking lot. All under a gray sky.

Dad lay there in his bed just as when we'd left him, the blanket still to his chin, eyes closed. The room seemed perhaps too bright for the morning light in through the vertical blinds, even with the overcast sky and the blinds closed all the way.

"Good morning, Bill," Mom said and set her purse on the chair against the wall, then kissed him on the cheek. "I hope you slept well," she said, and Dad answered, "Morning," the single word still strong, still calm.

Then Mom left to go find whoever was in charge, inquire again as to when his room would be ready, and those meds he was supposed to have, and when the doctor who'd admitted him might check in on him.

Melanie and I only stood in the room, neither of us sitting down.

We asked him questions, and he gave back single-word answers: "How are you?" "Tired." "Do you want the TV on?" "No." "Can we get you anything?" "Water."

I went to see if we could give him water and met an orderly out in the hall, who went to ask someone else, and I came back into the room.

Melanie smiled at me, her arms crossed, though the smile was a sorry one, a rueful one, a pitiful one. A sad smile.

He seemed not to be here. These questions we had for him, however clear and strong his single-word answers, seemed more an interruption than anything else. He was only answering us because he had heard questions.

Mom came back in with the orderly, who said he could have a little water and ice. Breakfast had been over for a while now, and lunch would be in a couple of hours. "He didn't eat anything," Mom said, "but the supervisor said the doctor told her that's nothing to worry about, it's the stress of moving in here that might be making him lose his appetite."

She had a Styrofoam cup in her hand and turned to the bed, and said, "Bill, here's some ice water."

But now my dad was struggling to sit up, was pushing back the blanket, eyes open. He had on a T-shirt and boxers, and said, "I need to go to the bathroom. I need to go to the bathroom."

The orderly stepped right in between Mom and Dad, and took Dad's arm to help him up.

Life

It was a struggle, this moment. My dad could not walk alone to the bathroom, couldn't, it seemed, sit up by himself anymore either. But the orderly helped him, the two of them inching across the three or four feet to the bathroom. All of it a struggle.

Mom had moved to the foot of the bed, the cup still in her hand. Melanie and I stood near the door. I remember I had my hands on my hips, watching. I remember Melanie had her arms crossed, and was watching too.

The orderly pulled the bathroom door closed behind them.

Mom turned to us, whispered, "You don't need to stay any longer. Brad and Joan are coming over in a while. They both have the day off for the Fourth, and we thought we'd just spend some time here."

"Okay," I said. "But we'll wait till he's out. I want to say goodbye."

She nodded, smiled up at me. "And the lavender farm. Don't forget."

"Stop worrying," I said. "We're going."

The door opened then, and the orderly helped Dad along, and here was another struggle, this time to get him back into the bed.

So very much more work than two days ago in the hospital, when Mom had helped him back into bed after our walk to the bluff looking out at the strait when he'd paused there in the work of lifting his legs onto the bed, and looked up at me, his eyes open wide, surprised, or angry, or just tired of everything, and said from nowhere, "I know I've done wrong things, but I know I've been forgiven. That's it."

"Bill, honey," Mom said, and turned from us. "Bret and Melanie are heading out now. They're going over to Tim and Bridget's."

The orderly was helping him try to ease back onto the bed. Dad's feet were up, but he was turning, it seemed, as though he might be trying to get out again.

"I'm glad we got to see you," I said from where I stood.

"Yep," Dad said, and now he was in fact leaning back, and Mom set the cup beside the TV on the dresser behind us, moved to the bed and started pulling up the blanket.

"Good-bye, Bill," Melanie said from beside me.

"Yep," Dad said.

And now he was back in place, his eyes closed, the blanket to his chin. The orderly stepped away, left the room, and Mom turned to us, smiled with her head tilted just the smallest way.

That was when Melanie stepped over to the bed and bent to his cheek, gave him a kiss, and said, "I love you."

"Yep," he said.

And I cannot make this up. I cannot make this up:

I went to the bed then, too, and bent to him, kissed him on the forehead. His eyes were closed, and stayed closed.

I stood, said, "We're heading out now, Dad."

"Yep," he said.

"I love you," I said.

"I love you too," he said. Clear and strong, calm and certain.

His eyes were closed, the blanket tucked to his chin.

We left then, because our vacation was almost over. We left, because we needed to get to Tim and Bridget's to visit, to hang out and talk, to have dinner tonight, and get to bed early because the flight home to Baton Rouge tomorrow was leaving so early, and we'd have to turn in the rental car at a lot a couple miles from the airport, then take a shuttle in, and then fly home. We left, because I needed on Thursday to head into the office for a few hours and do some work on the journal—I'd already been gone almost three weeks—while Melanie washed clothes because I'd have to pack and head out to Denver on Friday. We left, because on Saturday I'd have to write a talk I was to give that indicted the Christians I was there to help celebrate, and then fly the next day to Jerusalem and two more weeks of teaching.

167

Life

I left him there in the hospital room, because I had other things—so many other things, all of them about writing—to do with my own life.

But first we went to Jardin du Soleil.

In part to appease my mother, and because Melanie loved lavender—she had lotions and soaps and sachets at home—we drove down from the rehab center and back over the overpass and onto the main drag, then left onto the road that led out toward The Three Crabs.

A few minutes later here was the carved wooden sign, Jardin du Soleil, and we pulled into a gravel parking lot, spread before us wide fields of purple that eased down the hill and toward the tree line a few hundred yards away. Beyond it all the Olympics.

A gift shop stood to our left, gray wood siding and a peaked roof that made the building look more like a country church than anything else. Flowers in beds all around, lavender and poppies and sunflowers, all neat and perfect. To the right lay another garden, this one square and thirty feet across, surrounded by a purple and gray picket fence, inside it lavender planted in a circle around a large birdbath in the center.

And there were the fields: rows and rows of lavender, each bush its own eruption of color. Purple, and purple, and purple.

We stepped into the gift shop, a place cluttered with too much merchandise. A woman wearing a lavender apron stood behind a counter, working some small lavender bauble in her hands, and Melanie said, "Would it be all right if we walked down into the fields and just looked around a little bit? We can't make the festival and we're headed out of town."

The woman put down whatever it was she had in her hands, looked at us and smiled, nodded. "You just go right ahead," she said.

There is a photograph I took of Melanie standing in a row of lavender.

She has on a light blue jersey top, three-quarter sleeves. The lavender is waist-high, and she has a hand out and touching the blooms. She is smiling, though her smile seems a sad one. The sky above her is gray, the tree line far away behind her.

In a few minutes from when I took this picture we would go back into the gift shop and purchase some things, gifts for friends—lavender soap, a few small sachets, a vial of lavender oil you drip onto a light bulb to give the room that fragrance.

We'd drive away from Sequim to Sumner, across the Hood Canal Bridge and past Poulsbo, through Bremerton, across the Tacoma Narrows Bridge, and then into the driveway of Tim and Bridget's, where we will have a view of Mount Rainier, broad and snow-capped. From their front-room window the mountain seems a mile away, though it's almost forty.

We will hang out at their house a while, then head for their favorite Mexican restaurant down the road in Orting. It will be closed— this is the Fourth of July—and we will then wander through towns in the area, looking for open restaurants, finally ending up at an Olive Garden in Puyallup. We will head on back to their house then, and watch a television broadcast of the fireworks show out on the water in Seattle.

All this while, we four will talk about Dad, and about Mom. Melanie and I will tell them about how good Dad had seemed when we first got out there, about that cup of coffee, and the walk out to the bluffs, the drive on the back roads from Port Angeles back to Sumner and the rehab center.

But we will tell them too of how he seemed when we left.

Tim will tell us of how bad the doctors are out there, and of how distraught Mom has been at the therapy Dad was supposed to get, that hippie with the dirty house, cat hair everywhere and the weird smell of the place.

Then we will go to bed early, before 9:00, because Melanie and I have to get up at 4:00, head for the airport.

But when I took the picture, none of this had happened yet. I was only taking a photograph of my wife, whom I love.

Life

I had only a few minutes before spoken the last words I would speak to my father. I had told him I loved him, and he had told me he loved me too.

What had not yet happened had not yet happened.

But our last words to each other were—and what word is there? What word am I seeking to say what I mean? Me, who trafficks in nothing but words?

Correct. Our last words to each other were correct.

But is this true? Hadn't Melanie and I known he was somewhere else? Were his words back to me only his repeating me?

Or does this matter? This pondering of the meaning of words, when the words were in fact spoken?

When I think of this day, the last day I saw my father alive, it is this photograph of Melanie I think of first: her in a field of lavender at a farm in Sequim, Washington, a gray sky above her, a tree line far behind her.

And I remember what I said to my father, and what he said back to me.

16

I cannot sleep.

My father has died in Sequim, Washington, and I am in a room in Jerusalem.

I saw him only six days ago.

I am afraid, but I do not know of what.

I sit up in the dark, then turn, put my feet on the cool tile floor. But I do not stand, because there is nothing for me to do. According to the bedside clock, it is a little after 3:00. I have lain here unable to sleep for over five hours now.

Jackie was standing with Derek at the front desk when I came up from my room. I'd spoken to Melanie for twenty minutes or so, going over logistics she had already solved: she and Zeb would fly out tomorrow morning from Baton Rouge; Jacob, a sophomore at the College of Charleston, would fly up to Newark tomorrow afternoon, meet my flight in from Tel Aviv, and we two would fly together to Seattle, arriving after 11:00 tomorrow night. Melanie and Zeb would meet us at the food court at the airport, then we'd take a shuttle out to get a rental car. We'd stay at a hotel there in Seattle, then get up the next morning and drive back out to Sequim.

She'd already arranged this all, even down to the hotel, only a couple blocks from the car rental lot. The same one at which we'd dropped off a car five days before.

Derek—wiry, balding, and with a pale beard and wire-frame glasses—put out his hand for me to shake. He had on what seemed the same outfit he's had on every time I've seen him: a worn and soft long-sleeve denim shirt with the sleeves rolled up, a pair of light green khakis. He's a painter and has a studio in Yemen Moshe, the tightly packed neighborhood of high-end limestone homes and apartments that spills down the hillside right next door to Mishkenot. Last year we spent a good deal of time together—he and Jackie were the ones to take me to the Holy Sepulcher itself—and so seeing him is a kind of relief: he's a friend, too.

I shook his hand. "I'm sorry for your loss," he said, his British accent elegant and affable, his voice with the same quiet confidence I'd come to know last year. He's been here since 1973, moved from Newcastle as a young man "to see what was going on here," he once told me.

"Thank you," I said. "I'm sorry all this is going on. That all this has messed everything up."

"Stop," Jackie said. "No more of that." She smiled, put her purse strap over her shoulder. "ML and Andrea aren't in their rooms, so they must be out getting something to eat. We'll check in on them when we get back."

"Now let's get something ourselves," Derek said, and we left out the glass doors, and stepped into the warm desert air.

Life

The world outside had gone on working, as if nothing had happened at all. We walked up the sidewalk beside the curved street lined with limestone and past the iron gates, then along paved walkways through a large and landscaped civic garden of olive trees and rosemary, and out to the main street Shmuel had brought us in on.

Traffic was heavy, cars darting in and out and cutting each other off, horns honking. People walked along the sidewalks, pushed strollers, held hands, walked singly and in groups.

It was nearly dark, and we'd headed to the left, up the street I would one day know as Emek Refaim—Melanie and I would live in an apartment on this street, just across from Café Hillel, where I would write a large portion of the novel I would be working on then, getting up each morning and walking across the street at 7:00 when it opens to order my cafe hafuch—something like an American coffee—and park at a table, and write.

But this night I was in a foreign country walking a foreign street jammed with life. Beside us were brick and limestone homes set back from the narrow street a few yards, stone and iron fences out front of each, and I could see up ahead as we walked a small downtown of sorts: a couple traffic lights, some shops, restaurants, all fronting right on the street.

Traffic was even thicker here, people jammed even tighter, and I wondered at what was going on, then realized it was only this place's life, that nothing particular, as far as I could tell, might be happening at all. These were only people—families, couples, old and young—out on a beautiful summer night, the air even as we walked here losing its bright warmth and cooling, cooling. This was the desert, and this was the end of a day.

"Hummus?" Derek said to me over his shoulder in the midst of all this movement and life, Jackie walking beside me. I said, "That's great!" and Derek stopped right there at the first light we came to, and we waited with so many others for the light to change so that we could cross.

"Falafel Doron is a good place," Derek said beside me. "Nothing fancy at all, but they've got good hummus."

"This is German Colony," Jackie said. "I think we may be able to find an apartment here or in the surrounding area. It's a bit pricy, but the location is wonderful."

From where I stood there at the intersection, I could see a grocery store down the sidewalk to my left, three or four cafés on this side and across the street, a gelato store, a butcher shop, what looked like a stationery store. The sidewalks out front all jammed.

The light changed, and we surged with everyone else across the street, moved along the windows of a restaurant I thought perhaps was the one we'd be heading into. But we passed it, then stepped inside the next door down into what at home could only have been described as a hole in the wall.

Three cheap Formica tables, a few cheap chairs, and a reach-in Coca-Cola cold box were to the right, to the left the food counter with a short line of customers, at the end of it Derek, beside him Jackie. Behind the counter stood three men all working at assembling food, behind them the shawarma spit with its inverted pyramid of meat.

"What would you like?" Derek said, already at the counter, smiling. Jackie had her purse open and wallet out.

"Whatever you think's good," I said, and shrugged. "But hummus. And falafel."

We sat at a table—most everyone who came in to order was there for takeout—and talked while we ate. Up at the border with Lebanon it seemed a war was about to break out; their son, Jonzi, was in the army, and they were worried about what might happen were things to escalate up there. And there were still and always rockets being lobbed into Israel from the Gaza Strip. Derek told of an apartment in Yemen Moshe he'd gone to check out for us, but it had been too small and cost too much.

We talked, dipped pita into the bowl of hummus between us, nibbled at the falafel. The food was good—Melanie and I would make this our regular fast-food stop once we moved here—and then we walked on back to Mishkenot, night full upon us now, the streets still just as jammed.

Andrea's door was open, and we three stepped in from the atrium hallway. The double doors in the sitting room stood open, and we found Andrea and ML out on the portico, sitting in the two chairs for her room. They were eating watermelon they had bought at the grocer's in German Colony.

Andrea stood as soon as she saw me, set the slice of watermelon on the small table between their chairs. She was tall and a little thick, with curly hair and a loud voice. She hugged me, told me how sorry she was for my loss, and how sorry she was I wouldn't be teaching in the program, but that they'd have me back next year.

And then here stood ML, the poet professor from Wayne State I hadn't yet met. He wore chunky black glasses, and although his head was clean-shaven, he had a snow-white goatee grown nearly to mid-chest. He stood, said, "Bret, my brother, God bless you," and took hold of me, hugged me hard. "I'm sorry," he said.

He's been a friend ever since.

Derek walked down the portico to the next set of chairs, brought them back for Jackie and me, then sat down himself on the limestone step beneath Andrea's double doors, and we talked more: about teaching, and how ML and Andrea could make do without me, though I'd be missed; about the air strike by Israeli forces that day on the Gaza Strip, and yet more on what seemed about to happen up on the border with Lebanon; about apartments.

I ate a slice of watermelon, listened, said a few things here and there.

But my eyes were looking at the walls of the old city. At Jerusalem, just across the shallow valley from where we sat. In the night sky above it all a full moon.

It was a view I'd hoped to save for later. When I would be alone, finally, this day over. But here it was, now.

The walls were lit up like they always were at night, bright limestone-white walls weathered and leached with age stretching off to the left and parallel to the portico. The walls were movie-like, castle walls in the desert with square turrets every few hundred feet. This side, the west, was maybe a half-mile long, and I could see to the left and halfway down the Tower of David, the stone spire lit up just like the walls.

Directly out from the portico stood Mount Zion itself, and the lit-up Dormition Abbey. The old city walls did not encompass the mount itself, instead turned perpendicular away from us and toward the Temple Mount so that the abbey and the buildings atop Zion stood alone. Cars moved along the street at the base of the walls.

Here was Jerusalem, the Holy City.

And then I smelled something, a familiar smell, a good smell, and I looked from the walls to the landscaped garden area below the portico.

Every few feet a set of limestone steps led down from the portico to a landscaped garden area, where lay flowerbeds filled, I could see in the moonlight, with lavender in bloom.

"That's lavender," I said, and stood, went to the edge of the portico and down the steps, and I bent to the beds, pulled a single stalk, and smelled it: sharp, pungent, familiar.

I stood down there for a moment, looked at the walls, at that moon. ML and Jackie and Derek and Andrea were quiet behind me, only a few feet away up on the portico, but halfway around the world from me, right here in Sequim this very moment.

And then I turned, walked back up to the portico, sat down, and told them of a town named Sequim, and about seeing my father only six days ago, and about the Lavender Festival we had missed, and how it had seemed important—so very important—that Melanie and I stop at a farm that grew this flower before we left town.

Not long after, I left for my room. Jackie volunteered to walk me back down the hallway, and then I said goodnight, hugged Andrea and ML and Derek, thanked them for their company this night, told Andrea and ML I'd see them next summer, and Derek in a couple of months. At the door to my room, I gave Jackie a hug as well, told her how sorry I was to have to cancel teaching in the program, and how thankful I was she—a friend—had been there at the airport.

Once in the room, I called Melanie yet again.

We talked for a very long time. Whatever the telephone charge would be did not matter.

More details had come to Melanie by that time in a second phone call from Leslie, the first from her simply to inform Melanie of Dad's death. Leslie had told her now that there'd been no sign of change in Dad the rest of the week after we left: he'd continued to lie in bed there in the rehab center, answer questions full-voiced when asked, only move when he had to get up to go the bathroom. Then they'd brought him to the hospital Saturday for his scheduled round of dialysis, and the doctor had seen how bad his leg had gone, scheduled the amputation.

But a few minutes after eight Sunday night, Mom home to take a shower, Leslie in a chair by his bed, Dad had suddenly let out one long breath. Leslie went to him, though she already knew from the sound of that breath out that he had died.

She ran out into the hallway, screamed for a nurse. Once one and then another and then a doctor had made it to the room, they hadn't let her back in.

He died at 8:25.

Near nine Mom made it back to the hospital, Leslie meeting her out in the hall. By this time the staff had finished what they needed to finish in the room, and when Leslie brought her in, Dad still on the bed and covered to his chin, Mom broke down, yelled things at him, sobbed, collapsed.

No one had seen this coming. No one. He was in for the amputation of a leg, but he'd had internal bleeding—the doctor on call guessed he'd had a gastric ulcer that hemorrhaged, and because all eyes were on the leg and what would be happening there soon, no one bothered to check on his stomach.

When Dad's doctor came in for the amputation Monday morning, he'd found out only then Dad had died, and he met with Mom. "Your husband was not supposed to die," he told her.

All this from Leslie, through Melanie, to me.

Now I cannot sleep.

It is dark in the rooms, and I am alone, and the clock tells me it is still a little after 3:00 in the morning.

I have been awake since the morning after a speech I gave in Denver at which I alienated most of a large group of believers who work to write and to publish and to market books they believe helped Christians in their belief. I have been awake through a rush to the airport, and through a layover in Newark, and through the long flight here, and through *The Inferno*, and through the news brought to me of my father having died, spoken by my wife, who seems, as I think of it, the best person on the planet, in all of its history, to deliver such news.

I have been awake through the bustle of nightlife in German Colony, and through talk of war, and a slice of watermelon.

I have been awake through the majesty—I mean this word—of the walls of old Jerusalem at night, a full moon above them.

I have been awake through all this, and sleep seems pointless, a luxury afforded other people. Something I cannot attain this night.

And so, because I am alone, and because I am afraid, and because I know I am not going to sleep, and because, finally, I know nothing else to do, I stand from the bed, and walk across the cool tile floor into the sitting room, and to the double doors that let out onto the portico, and I open them.

Here are the walls, and the Tower of David, and Dormition Abbey, and Mount Zion itself, unencumbered by those walls. All lit up.

But the moon is gone now.

Life

I do not know what I am looking for in taking in this view at this moment.

At home in Baton Rouge it is only 8:30 last night, and I could call Melanie. In Sequim, it is 6:30. Still daylight.

But I am here. My father has died, and I am looking at the city where the history of faith I call my own is centered. I am looking at the place where the temple of all temples was built to house the name of God; I am looking at the city abandoned by God, and yet never abandoned by him; I am looking at the city where the resurrection of Christ occurred, where the beginning of all I know of mercy and forgiveness and renewal began, and where the assurance of eternal life—the life into which one you love is ushered once that loved one has died—was borne out by an event in history, witnessed by hundreds, influential in its concrete fact even to this day, the place where the fact above all facts occurred: Christ conquered death.

But my father is dead, and though he gave out an utterance as he struggled to climb back into a hospital bed in Port Angeles—"I know I've done wrong things, but I know I've been forgiven. That's it."—where now is my comfort, and where now is my assurance?

Why have I not yet cried at my father's passing?

A single car moves along the street down there at the base of the walls, its headlights casting out onto the pavement a thin and hollow answer of some sort, one I do not understand. Or, perhaps, this is no answer at all. This is only a car before dawn, someone on his way to work in Jerusalem.

Then I smell the good smell again, and I look down from these walls, from that road, the car already gone now, and see in the dark out here the lavender beds below me.

I go to the set of steps down from the portico—I am still barefoot, the limestone tiles out here rough and cold—and to the beds, where I kneel, then break off stalk by stalk by stalk a good dozen lavender blooms, each stalk a foot or so long, me filled with the mint and herb and sharp sweet smell of the flowers.

I pick them for my mother.

And then, when I believe I have enough for her to make a bouquet she can keep, a gift from her son who has been to Israel and back to bring her flowers that the fields surrounding her town are already filled with, I break off another dozen.

These will be for Melanie.

Who knows if they will make it through security at Ben Gurion or through customs when I get to Newark? It is the doing of this now that seems to matter. The intent of the gesture: its design, its import.

I know this is only a gesture—a move someone would make in a novel I was writing in order to represent something else, a move I know would be very difficult to pull off in words because it is so maudlin, so sappy, so cloyingly sentimental.

But I do it, because what else is there to this life but gesture? What is there beyond the act itself, the doing of something, to show love?

Words, yes. But words are deceitful, so scheming as to speak truth and untruth in the very same instant: in a book of words I wrote, my father is alive. But he is dead.

Acts are what matter. The act in the instant. This is what I have believed my entire writing life. This is what I mean when I exhort my students to *show* and not *tell*.

This is what I believe as a believer in Christ: for just as the body without the spirit is dead, so also faith without works is dead.

Give us gesture.

I stand and look at the thick handful of blooms in my hand, gray here in the dark, the moon somewhere else. I will wrap these in the newspaper on the desk back in the room. I will make a space for them in my backpack, slip them in and be as careful as I can not to crush them on the trip to Seattle.

This is a gesture. This is an intended moment.

This is all I have.

Life

Once I've wrapped the flowers in the newspaper, taken out from the backpack the extra shirt and pants I'd packed in there in case I lost my luggage getting here, and once I've settled in the backpack the foot-long package so that it's standing inside, and once I've turned off the lights I had to turn on to accomplish all this, I go back to bed.

But this time I don't even try to sleep. Instead, I take the remote from beside the clock on the nightstand—it's almost 3:30—and I turn on the television, run through channels broadcasting in Hebrew and Arabic, in Russian and Malay and German and French and Urdu and Italian. And English.

Here from the screen is the sudden burst into the room of a baseball stadium choked with roaring fans, a batter standing at home plate and swinging hard, and then the smooth and beautiful arc of the ball high into the night sky and beyond the wall in right field. The fans cheer even louder now, and I quickly turn down the volume until the sound is near nothing.

Yet the player doesn't run, only stands there at the plate, and for a moment I believe there is something wrong here, that this man has made a mistake by not loping away from home to make a victory turn past all the bases. Instead, he only squares himself up to the plate again, takes a practice swing, waiting for another pitch to come to him, and here it is: another baseball comes toward him, and the man at the plate hits this one as well, yet another home run.

And it comes to me: this is the Home Run Derby. This is the week of the all-star game, and I am watching the Home Run Derby, live from PNC Park in Pittsburgh.

I lay back in the bed and watch all of it, watch the crowds erupt with each hit that slams past the fence there in Pittsburgh. I watch the players in their brightly colored uniforms congratulate each other as they come away from home plate once they have finished the task of swinging at pitches, watch the spray of young kids in uniforms of their own in the outfield shagging balls that don't make it out of the park—the children of players and management, I imagine, given this honor—and I watch the commercials for Slim Jims and Gatorade and Nike and Red Bull and Coca-Cola and Chevy trucks. Then more home runs.

My father is dead.

And I am not sleeping.

I think of Dodger Stadium, and the games my dad took us to there when we were young, the winding drive up into the hills at sunset, the long trek from parking and into the stadium itself.

I remember the first time—I cannot have been older than six or seven—I emerged from a concrete tunnel into the surprise of how huge and bright this place was, the frightening fall away at my feet of steps down toward a perfect green field, where uniformed players no bigger than bottle caps played catch with each other in the outfield, far to my right home plate and a tiny crouched catcher, a pitcher just as small on the mound throwing a baseball at him.

And my dad in front of us and moving down and down, into the sea of seats and this crowd, and doing so without a look back at any of us to see if we were following.

17

Here are the people in the photo taken of us standing before my father's open grave at Ocean View Cemetery in Port Angeles, Washington: my brother Brad and his wife, Joan; their daughters Rachel and Alyson, who live just down the road in Sequim; my father's brother Lynn and his wife, Flo, up from Temecula, California; my mother, who lives in Sequim; my sister Leslie, her daughters Chloe and Isabel, her sons Marcus and Daniel, all of Camarillo, California; Melanie, our older son Zebulun, and I, of Baton Rouge, Louisiana, and our younger son, Jacob, who lives in Charleston, South Carolina; my brother Tim and his wife, Bridget, from Sumner, and Tim's children, Faith, from Huntington Beach, California, and Clayton, from Minneapolis, Minnesota; and my father's niece,

Life

Laura Coogan, daughter of his younger sister Anne, from Palos Verdes, California.

We are all well dressed and smiling. My mother has insisted on having the funeral director take this photo, and has insisted we all smile. She has never missed an opportunity for a photograph, is famous for pulling from her purse her camera—an Instamatic—and taking pictures of us, whether in restaurants or church or in line at Disneyland or in the living room watching television.

In front of us stands the metal railing and framework that surrounds the open hole of his grave. His casket is already settled at the bottom, though you cannot see this in the photo.

What you cannot see, either, is a low bench of black granite 30 yards or so to the right of Laura Coogan, the family member on the far right of the photo.

But I know it is there.

The funeral has been a sad affair. Not only for the event it marks, but for the paltry number of people who have attended: we twenty-one family members made up the vast bulk of those who came. The dozen or so others were friends Mom and Dad had made through church since they had moved up here three years ago, all of them their age. The pastor of their church, a man perhaps thirty-five years old, younger than any of us children, had only met my father in passing a couple of times and had to interview us to ask what he was like.

Tim gave the eulogy at the funeral home chapel, a small place on the Sequim side of town, before US 101 made it into somewhat congested, somewhat industrial, somewhat beat-up Port Angeles.

He kept things light, made us laugh: a good thing. He talked of RC Cola and how our lives were saturated with RC gear growing up, from beach towels to radios to baseballs to the bottles of soda pop we were all suckled with as infants; he talked of how gruff Dad could be, especially when it came to matters of his children doing yard work; he talked of how Sunday barbeques when we lived in Huntington Beach were the most important religious activity of his week.

And then we all came here, drove in a short line of vehicles through light after light and along business after business, past a paper mill on a spit of land that poked out into the Strait of Juan de Fuca. We followed the highway as it narrowed at the far end of town, then turned off into what seemed a residential area, then along more trees, and finally into a narrow driveway, and so into Ocean View Cemetery, and to one of the two plots Mom and Dad purchased not a month after I'd brought them here three years ago.

The pastor spoke a few more words, and my father's casket was lowered carefully, mechanically into the ground. Tim had brought a case of RC Cola to the graveside and passed out to each of us a can, and we all toasted my father, all of us sipping from our cans the sweet soda.

Now we have smiled for the photo.

As planned, Jacob met me in Newark, where we waited for our connection; dinner would be served onboard the plane.

He looked hard into my eyes when I first saw him and held him there in the terminal. He told me how sorry he was, and how sad he was that Grandpa was gone.

He was watching me for tears, I knew. But none came, and we only talked more about Grandpa, and this surprise.

Jacob and I met Melanie and Zeb as planned at Sea-Tac in the food court, where Zeb looked hard into my eyes. And Melanie, too. But still nothing came.

And as planned, we got our car from the rental lot, then drove a couple blocks to a cheap hotel, checked in—by that time it was after midnight, the drive out to Sequim two and a half hours and so too far to try this night—and we tried to sleep, we four adults in one room.

Life

Then, Wednesday morning, we drove to Mom and Dad's duplex behind the strip mall with its QFC, Swain's Hardware, that yogurt place. Everyone who is in the photograph was already there, our branch of the family the last to arrive. My mother came straight to me, and cried as I held her.

Later, once our bags were in the house, I carefully pulled from my backpack a bouquet of lavender wrapped in newspaper, and presented it to her. Here, in the light of day and in the swirl of all these people, and solidly inside the fact of our being here, the thin stalks of flowers seemed only enough for her.

"I brought you these all the way from Jerusalem," I told her, there in the kitchen. "Lavender. It's in bloom over there, too."

I hadn't known what I was looking for in handing them to her, hadn't known what the gesture I'd concocted what seemed a month ago might elicit.

She smiled at them, thanked me, hugged me, then set them on the counter, and carried on with what next she had in front of her: the pastor would be here any minute to talk to you children about your father, and where would you and Leslie and Brad and Tim like to sit to speak to him?

There was a viewing on Thursday. My father looked good, better than he'd looked in years. They'd performed an autopsy on him, and I'd wondered what that might mean, if it would affect how he'd look. I'd stood in the gravel parking lot outside the chapel with my children and with Melanie—we were the first to arrive in the line of cars leaving the duplex—and, coward that I am, let Tim and Brad and Mom and Leslie go in ahead of me before I entered.

But he looked good. Better than he had in years.

That was him, there. My father.

"That's his grave over there, right?" Tim says from beside me, the photo taken, the sextons working now to fill the grave. We are all still here, watching, and talking. Visiting. Waiting.

"Yep," I say, and don't turn toward that spot I led first Brad on a perfect blue-sky afternoon nine years before, then Melanie and Mom and Dad on a gray morning three years ago.

Tim leaves. The sextons continue their work.

Then my mother stands beside me. "Aren't you going to go over and visit his grave?" she says. "The writer?"

"No," I say. "Not today."

I say this, because today is about this man, here. My father.

Then Tim is beside me again. He says, "You know, there's a box over there. This metal box. And a notebook inside it." He is quiet a moment, then says, "Are you going to write something in there?"

I say, "I have already. When I was here before."

Tim says nothing. The sextons continue.

Then Tim says, "I wrote something."

I turn to him, see he is looking in the grave, slowly filling with dirt.

"What?" I say.

"About you," he says, and looks at me. He smiles. "And Dad. But about you. Being a writer."

"Good," I say, then, "Thank you," and I smile at him. Then we both turn to the grave, and watch, like the rest of the family, until the sextons pull sheets of green carpet over the bare dirt, and their work is finished.

I do not cry. But not, I believe, because I am unable to grieve.

It is because—I tell myself this—I do not yet know how to place what it is I am experiencing. I do not have the technique, the courage, the language to begin.

I do not yet know how to address this event, though only five nights before, on a misty street in Denver, I'd already begun.

You can't see my father's casket in the open hole before us in the photograph. And you can't see Carver's grave thirty yards or so to the right of Laura.

Life

But you can see past us how that whole side of the cemetery is open to the Strait of Juan de Fuca, deep blue water back there. You can see behind and to either side of us how trees have grown up from the bluff at the very edge of the grounds, but not in a way that blocks anything. Instead they frame that view, accent its beauty.

You can see, in this photo of my father's family, a sky huge and blue, but also traced this day with a thin band of gray clouds.

18

will have had

Three words—a mere grammatical form—I wrote in the margin of a student story on an evening in April 2008. But three words that led me, finally, to cry.

Only words, meant to express a tense, the fixing in time of a moment that has not yet happened, but which will.

There is no way to write this.

Even now, at this end of having tried to, I understand even more deeply how I do not have the technique, or the courage, or the language to achieve the story I want to tell.

But I am trying to write it, all the same. I am trying to tell a story, one that is as true as I can make it. A story I cannot make up. Nothing other than that.

There is lavender in this story. That is important. There is a man in a wheelchair in a courtyard just outside the window of my father's room, what may have been Gene Autry playing through the glass, above him a sky so blue I do not have the word for it. This is important as well. There are the old walls of Jerusalem at 3:00 in the morning, and an RC Cola salesman in Long Beach on a Saturday, leading his sons from a grocery store backroom out into the bright light of the store itself.

There is a story by an exchange student about the end of the world. A story that gave that man in Denver a way in.

There is a famous writer—a kind of father—and his grave. There is a real father, and his. And the view they both share: the final way in which the lives of Raymond Carver and my father intersect.

Today is December 31, 2010. My father died four years and 171 days ago.

It has taken me two years and seven months to write this. While doing so, I also wrote the next novel, the thirteenth book.

Zeb and Maggie have been married nearly two years now and live at Fort Meade, where Zeb, still in the army, works in satellite technology.

On August 27, 2010, their first child was born, Mikaila Jane. Melanie and I are grandparents.

Mikaila is the most beautiful baby I have ever seen.

Jacob has moved back to Charleston from Alexandria, and works for a Danish shipping company. He wears shiny leather shoes, creased pants, and dress shirts to work, and has an office with windows that look out toward the Ashley River. He has gone through two cars since Veronica's engine blew. And he has a serious girlfriend—the word *marriage* has been uttered of late—whom he met at a car meet in Virginia.

Melanie works part time at Chico's, a women's clothing store, for some extra money, and keeps up in every way she can on Mikaila, who will, a video Zeb and Maggie sent us this week attests, be able to roll herself onto her tummy any minute now.

In the evenings I sit in my leather chair in our home here in Hanahan, South Carolina, and mark up student stories.

But right now as I write this, my father is beside me in a car on a two-lane road between Port Angeles and Sequim. My mom is with us, and Melanie too. He is looking out his window, a Stim-U-Dent to his mouth, his elbow out in sunlight. Beyond him is a band of wildflowers, beyond that a field of pale green, beyond that the Olympic Range, holding close its snow.

Life

Right now, right now, there is me here at work, trying to make this all as good as it is within me to make it.

And what I see only now, in the long string of words I have here trafficked in, is how wrong I have been from the very start, from that moment on a Denver street, me talking to myself, believing I knew what this work before me would be.

This isn't an essay about the death of a father, but about the life of a son, living now on the other side of what has happened.

• • •

Works Cited in "At Some Point in the Future, What Has Not Happened Will Be in the Past"

Carver, Raymond. *Cathedral*. New York: Knopf, 1983.

_____. *What We Talk About When We Talk About Love*. New York: Knopf, 1981.

Gardner, John. *On Becoming a Novelist*. New York: Harper & Row, 1983.

Lott, Bret. *The Man Who Owned Vermont*. New York: Viking, 1987.

_____. *A Stranger's House: A Novel*. New York: Viking, 1988.

Selected Bibliography

Brautigan, Richard. "1/3, 1/3, 1/3," *Revenge of the Lawn: Stories, 1962–1970*. New York: Simon and Schuster, 1971.

Carver, Raymond. *Cathedral*. New York: Knopf, 1983.

_____. *What We Talk About When We Talk About Love*. New York: Knopf, 1981.

Gardner, John. *The Art of Fiction: Notes on Craft for Young Writers*. New York: Knopf, 1983.

_____. *On Becoming a Novelist*. New York: Harper and Row, 1983.

Lott, Bret. *The Man Who Owned Vermont*. New York: Viking, 1987.

O'Connor, Flannery. *The Complete Stories*. New York: Farrar, Straus and Giroux, 1971.

_____. *The Habit of Being: Letters*. Edited by Sally Fitzgerald. New York: Farrar, Straus and Giroux, 1979.

_____. *Mystery and Manners: Occasional Prose*. Edited by Sally Fitzgerald and Robert Fitzgerald. New York: Farrar, Straus and Giroux, 1969.

_____. *Wise Blood*. New York: Farrar, Straus and Giroux, 1962.

Schaeffer, Francis A. *Art and the Bible: Two Essays*. Downers Grove, IL: InterVarsity, 2006.

Notes

Why Have We Given Up the Ghost?

1. Henry T. Blackaby and Claude V. King, *Experiencing God: How to Live the Full Adventure of Knowing and Doing the Will of God* (Nashville: Broadman, 1994).
2. Rick Warren, *The Purpose Driven Life: What on Earth Am I Here For?* (Grand Rapids, MI: Zondervan, 2002).
3. Immanuel Kant, "An Answer to the Question: 'What is Enlightenment?'" in *Kant: Political Writings,* 2nd ed., ed. Hans Reiss, trans. H. B. Nisbet (Cambridge: Cambridge University Press, 1991), 54.
4. F. L. Cross, ed., *The Oxford Dictionary of the Christian Church* (London: Oxford University Press, 1958), 105.
5. Flannery O'Connor, *Mystery and Manners: Occasional Prose,* ed. Sally Fitzgerald and Robert Fitzgerald (New York: Farrar, Straus and Giroux, 1969), 43.
6. Ibid., 167.
7. Francis A. Schaeffer, *The Great Evangelical Disaster* (Westchester, IL: Crossway, 1984), 27.
8. G. K. Chesterton, *The Everlasting Man* (New York: Dodd, Mead, 1925), preface.
9. Ibid., 121–22, emphasis mine.
10. Flannery O'Connor, *The Habit of Being: Letters,* ed. Sally Fitzgerald (New York: Farrar, Straus and Giroux, 1979), 91.
11. O'Connor, *Mystery and Manners,* 156–57.
12. Ibid., 163.
13. Ibid., 171.

The Artist and the City, or, Some Random Thoughts on Why We Are Here

1. Henri-Marie de Lubac, *Paradoxes of Faith* (San Francisco: Ignatius, 1987), 48.
2. Catholic Information Network (CIN), http://www.cin.org/v2commun.html.
3. Ingmar Bergman, "The Dilemma of Filmmaking," *Hörde ni?,* no. 5 (May 1955).
4. Francis A. Schaeffer, *Art and the Bible: Two Essays* (Downers Grove, IL: InterVarsity, 2006), 65–66.

5. John Gardner, *On Becoming a Novelist* (New York: Harper and Row, 1983), 62.
6. John Gardner, "Redemption," *The Art of Living, and Other Stories* (New York: Knopf, 1981).
7. Schaeffer, *Art and the Bible*, 85–86.
8. De Lubac, *Paradoxes*, 48.

On Precision

1. Philip Levine, *The Bread of Time: Toward an Autobiography* (Ann Arbor: University of Michigan Press, 2008), 16.
2. John Gardner, *The Art of Fiction: Notes on Craft for Young Writers* (New York: Knopf, 1983), 7.
3. John Gardner, *On Becoming a Novelist* (New York: Harper & Row, 1983), 11.
4. Walker Evans, *Many Are Called* (New Haven: Yale University Press, 2004), 197.
5. Richard Brautigan. "1/3, 1/3, 1/3," *Revenge of the Lawn: Stories, 1962–1970* (New York: Simon and Schuster, 1971).
6. Richard Brautigan, *Trout Fishing in America* (New York: Dell, 1967).

Writing with So Great a Cloud of Witnesses

1. Bill Bryson, *A Short History of Nearly Everything* (New York: Broadway Books, 2003).
2. Franz Kafka, *Letters to Felice*, trans. James Stern and Elizabeth Duckworth (New York: Schocken, 1973), 156.
3. Raymond Carver, *What We Talk About When We Talk About Love* (New York: Knopf, 1981).
4. Flannery O'Connor, *Mystery and Manners: Occasional Prose*, ed. Sally Fitzgerald and Robert Fitzgerald (New York: Farrar, Straus and Giroux, 1969), 83.
5. John Steinbeck, *Working Days: The Journals of "The Grapes of Wrath," 1938–1941*, ed. Robert DeMott (New York: Viking, 1989), 29.

Humble Flannery

1. Flannery O'Connor, *Mystery and Manners: Occasional Prose*, ed. Sally Fitzgerald and Robert Fitzgerald (New York: Farrar, Straus and Giroux, 1969), 84–85.
2. David Madden, *Touching the Web of Southern Writers* (Knoxville: University of Tennessee Press, 2006), 75.
3. O'Connor, *Mystery and Manners,* 63–64.

4. Ibid., 159–60.
5. Flannery O'Connor, *The Habit of Being: Letters*, ed. Sally Fitzgerald (New York: Farrar, Straus and Giroux, 1979), 334–35.
6. O'Connor, *Mystery and Manners*, 107–8.
7. Ibid., 96.
8. Ibid., 34.
9. R. F. Christian, *Tolstoy: A Critical Introduction* (London: Cambridge University Press, 1969), 150.
10. O'Connor, *Mystery and Manners,* 68.
11. O'Connor, *The Habit of Being*, 143.
12. Flannery O'Connor, *The Complete Stories* (New York: Farrar, Straus and Giroux, 1971); *Wise Blood* (New York: Farrar, Straus and Giroux, 1962).
13. O'Connor, *Mystery and Manners,* 112.
14. O'Connor, *The Complete Stories*, 420.
15. Walter Sullivan, "In Time of the Breaking of Nations: The Decline of Southern Fiction," *Southern Review* new ser. 4 (April 1968): 299–305.
16. Miller Williams, "Remembering Flannery O'Connor," in *Flannery O'Connor: In Celebration of Genius*, ed. Sarah Gordon (Athens, GA: Hill Street Press, 2000), 3.